CALIFORNIA RANCHO DAYS

by Helen Bauer

CALIFORNIA STATE SERIES

Published by
CALIFORNIA STATE DEPARTMENT OF EDUCATION
Sacramento, 1957

ACKNOWLEDGMENTS

The author wishes to express her genuine appreciation for all assistance given in the collection and compilation of this material. In a project of this kind when written material on the subject is at a premium, it is necessary to seek out original sources of information. The descendants of early California families, the officers of historical societies and county officials from all parts of California have been cooperatively interested and generously responsive. To all of these and to many others whose names are too numerous to mention individually, I hereby acknowledge my indebtedness and sincere gratitude.

For the pictures of rancho life, generous credit is given to Arthur Barr, Pasadena. Hubert A. Lowman, Covina, merits my grateful acknowledgment for pictures of present-day adobe rancho homes. Pictures were secured and credit hereby given to: Karl Obert, Hal Boucher and Shreve Ballard of Santa Barbara; the Security-First Natl. Bank, Title Insurance & Trust Co. and the Los Angeles Times of Los Angeles.

Special appreciation is expressed to Albert J. Dunkel, Audio-Visual Education Section, Los Angeles City Schools, for his competent ability in making the drawings, maps and brands.

To the editorial staff of the publisher for their valuable editorial assistance.

With all these, one must still acknowledge the help, understanding and cooperation of family members, which is given generously to my husband and children. My son, Sherwin J. Carlquist, merits and deserves an added measure of gratitude for being my helpful critic and constant source of inspiration.

printed in
CALIFORNIA OFFICE OF STATE PRINTING
SACRAMENTO   4TH PRINT   6M   1964

AUTHOR'S FOREWORD

There are few places that have so rich and colorful a history as California. This story tells about the days of the ranchos. These days began with the missions and ended about the time that California became a part of the United States. Nearly every town and city in California was once part of some old rancho. The names of some of the ranchos are known to us today as towns or streets in our towns and cities. This story begins with the ranchos in the southern part of California. It ends with the story of ranchos in the northern part of the state.

You will want to find out the history of ranchos in all parts of California. You will want to see some of the old adobe homes and buildings that are still left. You will be glad that these buildings are left for all to see and enjoy. Some of them have been here since the flags of Spain and Mexico flew over California. Parts of ranchos are still owned by a grandson or great-grandson of early California rancheros.

The history of Spanish and Mexican California is largely the story of families who lived at that time. Almost every family and every rancho would make an interesting story. This book can tell only a few stories of families who lived then and what they did. Each story tells about some part of rancho life.

CONTENTS

HOW THE RANCHOS BEGAN
AND WHAT BECAME OF THEM

Have you ever seen an old California map? If you have, you might have seen a line that looked like a long road. This was El Camino Real (The Royal Highway). It was the highway of the padres between the missions from south to north. You would have seen two dots that were the first pueblos. They were Los Angeles and San Jose. You would have seen a few dots that were the presidios where the soldiers lived. These presidios grew into the cities of San Diego, Santa Barbara, Monterey, and San Francisco. Small Indian villages along the rivers, mountains, and ocean did not show on that map.

Not long after that the map of California began to look like a quilt. What were these large pieces of land here and there? They did not belong to the missions or the Indians. They were the ranches, or ranchos, as they were called. Those who lived on the ranchos were called rancheros. The first rancheros in California were Spanish soldiers. Many had come to California with the explorers. Some of them had come to help build the missions, pueblos, and presidios. Some of the soldiers finished their time in the army. They were free to go back to Spain or Mexico. Many of them chose to stay in California. The King gave them land to use as their own.

The ranchero had to have a home for himself and his family. What could be done without a builder and no one to show him? Many times the ranchero had to do the building himself. Usually, Indians from one of the missions came to help him. They had been taught by the padres how to make adobe bricks. Wood was brought from the mountains. It was needed for the roof and frames for the door and windows. Tule grasses were put across the wooden beams. Sometimes tar, or *brea*, was put on top of the roof. Later tile roofs were made for the larger houses.

In the very early days, rancheros built only small homes. Sometimes a house was

5

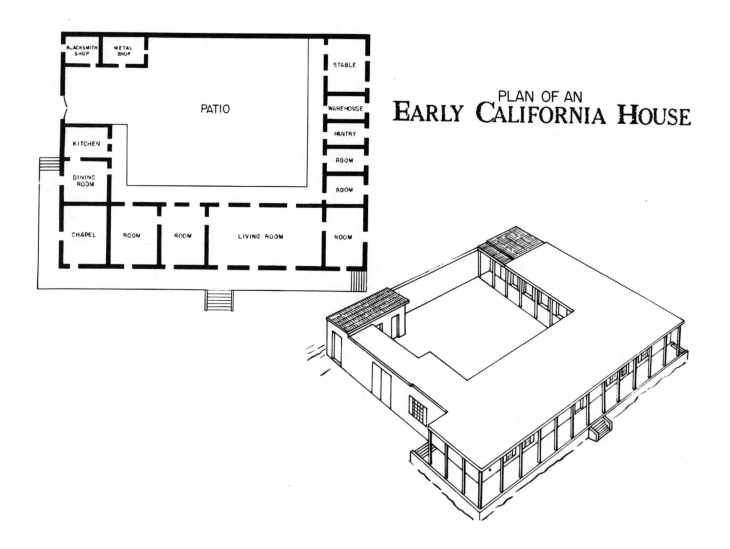

PLAN OF AN
EARLY CALIFORNIA HOUSE

BLACKSMITH SHOP

METAL SHOP

PATIO

STABLE

WAREHOUSE

PANTRY

ROOM

KITCHEN

ROOM

DINING ROOM

CHAPEL

ROOM

ROOM

LIVING ROOM

ROOM

built with only two rooms, a bedroom and a dining room. As the family grew larger, the ranchero added bedrooms. When he became richer, a large *sala,* or living room was built. Most of the cooking was done outside in the patio or courtyard. Almost every home was built around the patio. It was here the family liked to live and enjoy life. Friends came to visit there. It was the place where they danced and sang by the hour. A shady tree or a fountain made the patio a cool place. Strings of red and green peppers hung on the whitewashed walls. In the fall, yellow pumpkins and gourds were there. Flowers were always in bloom. The rooms inside were dark and gloomy. But the patio was a happy, bright place!

The rancho was a very busy place. But the people were not in such a hurry as we are today. The ranchero awakened early to give orders for the day. The Doña could be heard singing a sunrise song. The family all joined in the song of thanksgiving. The ranchero then stood on the porch to tell the *mayordomo,* or manager, what had to be done. There were hundreds of Indian men who helped with the cattle. They were not called cowboys in those days. The Spanish name *vaquero* meant the same thing. After a simple breakfast, the *mayordomo* and the *vaqueros* rode off toward the hills. In the afternoon, the ranchero rode on his fine horse to look over his lands and herds. He had to see that all went well on his rancho. Perhaps he galloped over to another rancho to visit with his friends.

Indian women helped with the work in the house. The Doña taught them to cook the Spanish food. They spun wool into thread and wove it into cloth. Some were taught to sew. None of the Indians were given money for their work. What would they do with money? Did not the ranchero give them food, clothing, and a place to live?

All Californians of early days spoke the Spanish language. Their dress, their homes, and their customs were Spanish. They no longer called themselves Spaniards or Mexicans. "We are in California," they said. "We are Californians now!" The women were gay and had kindly manners. The men were brave and always polite. The children were full of fun but spoke in low, soft voices. Most of all, they showed great respect for their

7

parents. The Californians were just as kind to strangers as to friends. Travelers knew they would be welcome day or night at any rancho. The stranger might stay as long as he liked. Sometimes, when he was ready to go, a fresh horse was given to him. Everywhere, there was the same carefree life. Pleasure was always first! Visitors said, "They are the happiest people on earth." Their time was spent in a round of feasting, gaiety, and happiness! Everyone had plenty to eat and drink. If he didn't, his neighbor gave him some of his. This was the Spanish period in old California.

There came a time when the peace and happiness of Spanish California were disturbed. The Mexicans felt unfairly treated by Spain. The Spanish kings wanted too much tax money. The people of California were too far away to know what was happening. One day in 1822 a ship came from Mexico to tell them the news. The message said that California belonged to Mexico, not to Spain. It made little difference to California which flag flew over it. The officials promised to be loyal to Mexico. By this time the missions had grown great. They had rich rancho lands around each mission. Mexico now said that the Church did not own the mission lands. Most of the padres left. Finally the missions and rancho lands around them were sold or given away.

Now there was more land to give to rancheros. There had been about twenty ranchos during the Spanish days. Half of them were within a hundred miles of the pueblo of Los Angeles. A few years later there were hundreds of ranchos given to those who wanted them. Any loyal citizen could ask for land. There were English, Scots, and Americans who asked for land too. They had to marry Mexican citizens or become Mexican citizens themselves. They had to belong to the Catholic Church. Under the new law of Mexico, anyone who wanted land had to ask the governor for it. He could ask for as much as 50,000 acres! He could not ask for less than 4500 acres. He had to tell how much land he needed for his family and cattle. He had to say that no one else owned the land. Usually he wanted a rich piece of land near water. He wanted hills nearby where the cattle could graze. A simple map of the land had to be sent to the governor in Monterey. The *alcalde*, or mayor, of the pueblo also had to say he could have the land.

Every rancho had a name. Today we call ranchos something like Lazy G or Diamond Bar —. The rancheros gave their ranchos names that had a meaning. Sometimes the rancho had a saint's name, like Santa Anita. One rancho was called El Encino (The Oak) because of a large oak tree on it. Rancho Rodeo de las Aguas stood for "Gathering of the Waters" because there were springs of water there.

The "golden years" of the ranchos lasted about fifteen years. As time went on, the rancheros grew richer and richer. They did not have lots of money. They were rich in many other ways. They were rich in the happiness of their homes and families. They were rich in land and cattle. Ships brought goods they needed in exchange for hides and tallow. All they wanted was to live—and they did it well. These were the days the Californians never forgot!

But a change was coming to California. More and more Americans were coming every year. In 1844 John C. Frémont, who had been sent by the United States to explore the West, traveled through California. In some of the settlements there were fearful whispers. Some said an army was on its way from Mexico. Others thought that all Americans were to be driven out of California. The Americans decided to do something themselves. One Sunday in June 1846, thirty-three Americans marched to Sonoma in the north. They knew that General Mariano Vallejo was a leader of the Californians. They went to his home and made him their prisoner. Then they were not sure what to do next. Should they raise the American flag? They wanted to take down the Mexican flag. "Let's make a flag that belongs only to California," they said. Someone found a piece of white cloth. A bright red star was painted in one corner. A brown grizzly bear was painted in the center. Someone found a piece of red cloth and put it along the bottom. On the flag the words, "California Republic," were printed. Soon the California flag floated out over the plaza of Sonoma. And the Bear Flag is the state flag of California today!

A few days after this happened in Sonoma, news came by ship that the United States and Mexico were at war. Three ships sailed into Monterey Harbor. Before the people knew what had happened, the United States flag was flying over the presidio at Monterey.

The same thing happened at San Francisco, at San Jose, and at Sutter's Fort. When the men at Sonoma heard the news, they pulled the Bear Flag down. Then they joined General Frémont's men who were marching south to Monterey.

Everything happened so quickly, the Californians did nothing. Commodore Stockton of the United States Navy took charge. He sent Frémont and his men by ship to San Diego. It was Stockton's plan to take Los Angeles himself. Pio Pico, the Mexican governor, had moved the capital from Monterey to Los Angeles. When he heard the Americans were coming, he fled to Lower California.

After the American flag was raised at San Diego, Frémont's men marched north again. Commodore Stockton met them in Los Angeles. Together they took possession of the pueblo. Not a single shot was fired. Leaders of the Spanish-Californians, José María Flores, José Antonio Carrillo, and Andrés Pico, brother of the governor, promised not to fight the Americans. All seemed very peaceful. Stockton and Frémont believed them and went back to Monterey. Sixty Americans were left to guard Los Angeles.

No sooner had Stockton and Frémont gone than promises were forgotten. The Spanish-Californians decided to regain Los Angeles. Captain Gillespie and the Americans fled to a hill near the plaza. Captain Gillespie knew he had to get help at once from Monterey. A very tall, thin man named John Brown (Juan Flaco) offered to go. Messages were written on thin papers. Juan Flaco hid them in his hair. He risked his life to ride the three hundred miles to Monterey. After the wild ride he was told that Stockton was in San Francisco. Poor Juan! On he went, until after another long ride he gave Commodore Stockton the news.

Stockton acted quickly. He sent a ship with men to San Pedro at once. There they met Captain Gillespie waiting with his soldiers. Now the three hundred men started toward Los Angeles. That night they camped at the Domínguez rancho. This time Andrés Pico and Juan Flores were watching—and waiting. They played a trick on the Americans. They had rounded up hundreds of wild horses. When the Americans came in sight, they saw great clouds of dust. "It looks like a thousand horsemen, doesn't it?"

asked Andrés Pico. "Yes," said Juan Flores, "they do not know that there are only a few men on those horses! But look, Andrés, our plan worked too well. The Americans have gone back to their ships. Oh well, they may come back—but they may not! Until they do, let's go back to a fiesta in Los Angeles!"

The American ship went south to San Diego. Commodore Stockton was not worried. He expected other American soldiers from the East. But there were only a hundred men who came. They were tired, hungry, and not ready to fight. They stopped to rest near San Diego. Andrés Pico was there ready to meet them with his lancers. What chances did Americans have against sharp lances on long poles? Some of the men were killed; many were hurt. This was the Battle of San Pascual. Kit Carson, the famous scout, slipped away at night for help. Soldiers from San Diego led the Americans to safety. Andrés Pico and his California soldiers raced back to Los Angeles again.

Commodore Stockton made up an army of sailors and soldiers. "This time all must fight!" he said. "And we must win!" Back they headed for Los Angeles. They hoped to hold it this time. The Americans had the north and San Diego. Frémont was on his way to take Santa Barbara. "Los Angeles—and then California is ours!" the soldiers said.

Flores and Pico were waiting again. This time the battle was by the San Gabriel River (near present-day Whittier). Again the Americans were met by the pointed lances. But this time the Americans were ready with guns. Pico and Flores saw that the Americans had won the battle. Even then they did not give up. The next day there was another battle. It was fought on a flat plain (East Los Angeles) called a *mesa*, or tableland. A thousand Californians came riding from the pueblo. Little flags of all colors were flying from their lances. Trumpets and bugles were playing! But the Californians did not win. Guns were fired right and left at the lancers. Andrés Pico and his men knew the war was almost over. He knew the Americans would have all of Californian soon. His soldiers were ordered back to the pueblo. Now it was easy for the Americans to march into Los Angeles and raise the American flag.

Pico and Flores sent a peace offer to Commodore Stockton. He sent back a harsh

11

answer. "If either of you is caught near here, you will be shot!" General Flores left for Mexico. But Andrés Pico worked out his own plan. He had heard that General Frémont was marching from the north. His game was to meet Frémont before the Americans did. When Frémont's army reached Cahuenga Pass (near Hollywood) he was there to meet it. This time Pico did not want to fight—he came to give up. Frémont did not know what had been happening in the south. So he was glad to make peace with Pico. On January 13, 1847, they signed a paper that ended California's part of the war. This was the beginning of American California. One year later, in February 1848, the United States made peace with Mexico. It was not until September 1850 that California was made the thirty-first state of the Union.

While all this was happening, gold was found in the north near Sutter's Fort. People began coming to California from all over the United States and other countries. By the end of 1849 there were thousands of new Californians. Miners returned from the gold fields. Many had not found the gold they wanted. Now they looked for something else. They saw the great ranchos. There were many acres of land where no one was living. "Why not stay here and live?" they thought. They did not know that the land belonged to someone else. When they found out, they did not care. They forgot that someone had been living there a hundred years before they came. Those who stayed on the land were called "squatters." They went to the American courts. They said they had found the land and now owned it. Others said they had bought the land. Some said the land had been given to them. It was not long before the Spaniards and Mexicans lost all or part of their ranchos. They did not understand the new American ways. Many Californians did not speak English and knew little about the law. One law told the ranchero to show papers to prove he owned the rancho. Two years were given him to do this. Most of the rancheros had no papers to show the court. Perhaps they had been lost long ago. Others had papers that showed boundaries that were gone. A pile of stones or an oak tree had once marked the corners. Who could prove a boundary line like that after so many years? Other rancheros had papers but did not think they had to show them. When the two years were up, many ranchos were lost.

Some of the rancheros did have papers to show the court. But they had to wait and wait. Some families waited for thirty years! Many of the old rancheros died before word came about the land. Often the sons sold the land for a few dollars. Then came the dry years when no rain came. This was in 1864 and 1865. Cattle by the thousands died all over the state. The ranchero had to have money. He borrowed from the Americans, but he could not pay the money back. Land was lost to the one who had let him have the money. Some of the land was sold for as little as twenty-three cents an acre! Within five years almost all the ranchos had new owners. Some of the rancheros went to live in the pueblos. Pueblos grew into towns. Towns grew into cities. What happened to the ranchos after rancho days makes another story.

California has not forgotten the old rancho days. Every month in the year there is a celebration of old days. Santa Barbara has the "Old Spanish Days." Monterey celebrates with a *merienda* each year. There are rodeos and fiestas in towns and cities all over the state. Even though California rancho days are gone, these celebrations bring back the gay life of that time!

JUAN BANDINI
THE FAMOUS DANCER OF SAN DIEGO

San Diego seemed to be first in everything! Explorers found the quiet bay before any other bay in California. Ships coming up the coast of California stopped at San Diego first. On Presidio Hill in San Diego there is a cross with these words, "Here Father Serra first raised the cross. Here began the first mission, here the first town, San Diego, July 16, 1769."

One of the first soldiers to build a home outside the presidio walls was Captain José Estudillo. It was built at the corner of the little plaza (now San Diego Old Town). At another corner of the plaza, Don Juan Bandini built a long, one-story house. One day word passed from one to another, "Don Juan has built a home for his bride, Dolores Estudillo. It is all finished and there is to be a *fandango* there tomorrow!" they said. "And what is more—there is to be a feast at noon for everyone! No one will want to miss this celebration!" And very few did! The large *sala* could hardly hold all who came. And there was dancing all that day and that night. Everyone knew that Don Juan was never happier than when dancing.

Juan Bandini had a rancho as well as a home by the plaza. His land was near the Mexican border. He was proud to have land, but he did not care to be a ranchero. Sometimes he rode north to the pueblo of Los Angeles. His good friend, Don Abel Stearns, was always glad to welcome him there. "Come be a partner here in my store," Don Abel urged. So it was agreed that he would. But Don Juan was much too busy to stay and work there. He had people to see and things to do from Mexico City to Monterey. "Don Juan is an important man," his friends said. "He seems to belong to the whole state!" While Don Juan was on one of his visits, Indians came to his rancho. Everything he had was stolen. Nothing was left of the home but smoking ruins. What could be done then?

14

His family did not wish to stay in the south. So he asked for and was given Rancho Jurupa near Los Angeles (now Riverside).

About this time, Don Abel Stearns met Don Juan's daughter. Arcadia Bandini was still very young. Don Abel was now forty years old! He thought her the most beautiful girl in California. "She is the queen of the señoritas!" he said. "And Don Abel is a fine businessman, better than all the others," Arcadia told her father. Everyone who heard about it laughed at the idea! But finally Don Juan said that Arcadia could marry Don Abel. The *vaqueros* made up a song about the two. Each verse ended:

> "Two little doves sang in a laurel,
> How lovely Doña Arcadia!
> How ugly Don Abel!"

The Estudillo house still looks out over the plaza in Old Town

But the marriage was a happy one for Arcadia. Don Abel built her the finest home in Los Angeles. Everyone called it El Palacio (The Palace) because it was so large. Every important person in the state came to visit there.

When Don Abel and Doña Arcadia had a *fandango* in their home, Don Juan was usually there! "He is the best dancer of them all!" people said. "He is even the best dancer in all of California! And don't forget—it was Don Juan who taught us how to waltz! He learned it in South America before he came here." When he took the floor everyone stood still and watched. His small feet seemed never to touch the floor! "I will be the dance master," he said. "Of course—he always is!" people whispered. "Who else could be?"

Two lines were formed facing each other. Then in time to the slow music everyone there danced the *contradanza*. Usually someone played the guitar. It was easy to find someone who played a violin. "Now a more lively tune!" Don Juan called, and the guitars sang out. "Come dance, my Arcadia!" Clapping in time with the music, he led his daughter to the center of the room. She danced with a glass of water on her head (*El Son*). She had a loop around her ankles. Usually not a drop of water was spilled. A shower of coins fell at her feet. "Ah, that was perfectly done!" Don Juan said proudly.

"Now the *Sombrero* (Hat) dance!" he called. A señorita danced so gracefully that men put their hats on her head. They piled one on top of the other until she could hold no more! As they did, they sang:

> "Take my *sombrero*—then I will feel
> Like a king who has crowned his queen!"

And the dancing señorita replied:

> "I like your *sombrero*
> Even better than a crown!"

The young men thought this lots of fun. The señorita's fun came later. Each young man had to pay a coin to get his hat back again!

16

Some of the dances were like games and were just as much fun! Often while they danced, nonsense verses were sung. In the *Fandango,* someone would suddenly shout, *"Bomba!"* (Listen!) Then hands were joined as in a game and verses sung, as:

"Now I see a rat,
Now I see many,
Some have big ears,
Some haven't any!"

"Now let's have a dancing game for children!" called Don Juan. "Soon they must go to bed." Then there was the waving of handkerchiefs and jumping about. Everyone laughed! After the children went to bed, others danced on and on! No one seemed to tire! Finally, one by one, everyone left. The music and the laughter faded away. Don Juan was usually the last one to go!

Those were happy days in California. Then in 1846 came the war between Mexico and the United States. Don Juan Bandini was in favor of the United States. "I believe the Americans will win the war," he said. "I think it will be better if they do." It was not only because his daughters had married Americans. "I think the Americans will have better government for us in California. The governors from Mexico have not always been good ones. Mexico has been too far away to know what we need. Perhaps the Americans will give us schools. We need more good roads. We need many things. You watch—when the Americans come—California will grow and grow!" So, Don Juan was friendly to Americans. He was willing to help. His neighbor, José Estudillo, did not feel that way. "I like them too," he said, "but we must not turn against the mother country."

When the American soldiers from the East came near San Diego, they found Don Juan and his family on a rancho nearby. "Help us," they said. "Give us cattle, horses, and grain." Don Juan promised to give what he could. Oxcarts were loaded until they could hold no more. Then he made ready to take his family to San Diego. The Bandinis rode

The Bandini house was once the center of life in Old San Diego

horseback, with extra horses trailing along behind. An American captain led the way. "I think the American officer—Commodore Stockton—will be glad to see us coming!" said one of the girls. "Why shouldn't he? Horses, loads of grain, and beans for the soldiers!" replied the captain. Then said a Bandini girl, "Perhaps we should have an American flag! Since you have none with you, we must make one!" Quickly, the mother and sister sewed one together. So the Bandinis came into San Diego. There was the screeching of heavy oxcarts. Dogs barked at the line of horses. And at the head of all was the new American flag flying proudly!

After the Americans came, San Diego did grow. But many years later it was decided that San Diego grew up in the wrong place. "San Diego is not even close to the bay!" some said. "No ship can land closer than three miles from the town!" "But," said others, "there is no water over by the bay. Yes—and we'll probably never get any there either. It has been tried before." But there were some who thought it could be done. "We'll try until we do get water there," they said.

So it was decided that the new part of San Diego would be by the bay. Now the town really began to grow. Some still liked Old Town. "Where shall we build—Old Town or New Town?" they asked. About that time there was a fire in Old Town. That settled it! After that, people knew that New Town would be the real city.

At that time, San Diego had twenty-nine ranchos. Most of them have become cities, towns, large fruit orchards, and farming centers. Some of the old rancho homes are almost the same as they were in rancho days. Some of the famous houses are still left in San Diego Old Town. Old Town seems far away from busy San Diego, now a large city by a beautiful bay. Whaling, supply, and trading ships used to anchor there. Now one sees fishing boats and sailboats, large and small. Hundreds of gray navy ships and merchant ships sail in and out. And this is the bay where the story of California first began!

JUAN DOMÍNGUEZ
WHAT THE TRADING SHIPS BROUGHT TO RANCHO SAN PEDRO

Many years before rancho days, the explorer, Juan Cabrillo, sailed up the California coast. As he came near present-day San Pedro, he saw plumes of smoke from Indian fires. So he named the place the Bay of Smokes. Another explorer, Sebastián Vizcaíno, gave it another name. His ships dropped anchor on St. Peter's Day. So he called the wide bay with the yellow cliffs San Pedro Bay.

Gaspar de Portolá was sent by Spain to find places for presidios or forts. With him was Pedro Fages, captain of the leather-jacket soldiers. His soldiers wore thick leather jackets to protect them from Indian arrows. Many of these leather-jacket soldiers later became California's first rancheros.

The leather-jacket soldiers saw fine herds of cattle in the fields. They were surprised at the fine crops, orchards, and vineyards on the mission lands. They thought of the time they would be soldiers no longer. "Why could we not have some of this rich land?" they asked. When they finished their time in the army, they were free to go back to Mexico or Spain. But some of them did not want to go. They wished to own land instead, and so they went to see the governor. Captain Fages, head of the leather-jacket soldiers, was now governor. He wanted to help the soldiers who had come with him. He wrote to Mexico saying, "There are several soldiers here who wish to own land in California. One of them has two hundred head of cattle. His name is Juan José Domínguez. I wish to let him have the right to use some of the land." Finally the answer came that he could have the land. So Governor Fages really started the rancho days in California. And Don Juan Domínguez was the first ranchero!

"There are several things you must remember, though," said Governor Fages. "Your land must be at least four leagues away from a pueblo, a mission, or an Indian village.

20

A house must be built on the land. You must always have at least 150 head of cattle. Besides that, there must be enough *vaqueros* to take care of the cattle." Juan Domínguez was sure he could do all these things. So he became the owner of Rancho San Pedro. His rancho had fine pasture lands in all directions. The harbor was nearby. The San Gabriel River was on one side. The little three-year-old pueblo of Los Angeles was not far away. What was more, he had 75,000 acres for his rancho! "What more could I want?" he asked.

For a while Don Juan had to stay as a soldier at San Diego. A *mayordomo* took care of his rancho for him. Then the day came when he was ready to leave San Diego. He had cattle there that he wished to take with him. One morning he said, "Come, *vaqueros*! We have a long journey. We have to drive my cows to Rancho San Pedro in the north. Now I am going to be a ranchero!" said Don Juan José. "I have been given many acres of land to use. I am going to build houses on my land. Is that not important? Spain must have builders as well as soldiers! Come now—let's be on our way!"

By the time Don Juan came to live on the rancho he was getting old. He did not do as much as he had planned. Days passed quietly and peacefully. But at the Bay of San Pedro there was always something exciting happening because of trading ships. The Spanish law said, "Only Spanish ships may land in California ports." Once in a while strange ships came. They were ships from Boston, on the other side of the United States. They had come all the long way around South America. At first they came to hunt otter along the coast. Then they found a way to fill their ships with otter skins without hunting for them. A ship would come from Boston loaded with things the Californians needed. There would be food and tools and cloth. The ship would anchor far out from the shore. At night there was a splashing of small boats. "There," said the captain, "the boats are loaded. Take care! We do not wish to be seen! Lower away—and quiet! They punish smugglers here, you know!" "Ay, ay!" said the sailors. But they were not afraid. Very few smugglers had ever been punished even if they were caught! They knew the Californians would be glad that the trading ships had come! Why? Because they gave the people the things they needed.

Near the house great kettles were smoking with crackling fires. It was here the fat was melted for tallow.

Blocks of tallow were weighed by the ship's captain

The boats rowed quietly to the shore. Men were waiting there in the dark. Sometimes there were Indians from the mission. Sometimes there were rancheros. Merchants came from the pueblo of Los Angeles. Each one wanted something from the Boston trading ship. "Have you any otter skins?" the sailors would whisper. "Yes—we have! Here is a bundle of fifty skins!" "How much do you want?" A price was named, but no money was paid. Instead, they were given goods worth about the same amount as the otter skins. The boat slipped back as quietly as it came. The Californians went back with the things they wanted. This trade of otter skins went on for years. Later they traded for hides and tallow. No one seemed to care. If anyone did, he said little about it. Others said, "If Spain only knew, the law about trading ships would be changed!"

A secret harbor that the Americans liked was a quiet bay at Santa Catalina Island. It was a place where a ship could anchor easily. At night the small boats could slip across the water to San Pedro. The Americans could trade not only with the Californians but with the Indians as well. The Indians traded otter skins for whatever they could get. They even helped the sailors clean the ships. The sailors went swimming and hunting. "Ah—next to being a sailor—this life is the best!" they said. When they left the island they usually sailed to China. They took a load of sea-otter skins and traded them for a high price. When they left China, they had a shipload of Chinese silks, shawls, combs, and dishes. Some of these things were taken to Boston to be sold. Many things were kept to take back to California to get more sea-otter skins and hides. Sometimes the trip all the way around took three years.

After California became a part of Mexico, trading was different. Word came to Boston, "California is ruled by Spain no longer. There are new laws. Any country can go there to trade now!" The Boston people, sometimes called Yankees, knew just what to take to California. They lost no time when they heard the news. Good strong ships were made ready for the trip. "Trade these goods for hides in California," the Yankee merchants said. "Take tools for farms. Take shoes and cotton goods. Everyone will want them. California women will love the shawls and silks from China. Be sure to take them!" So the traders learned what was best to take on the long trip.

23

When a ranchero heard a ship had come to San Pedro, the news spread for miles around. The mission and the ranchos usually had some hides and tallow stored away. Now everyone hurried to get more ready at once! Cattle were driven to the butchering place. Some of the meat was put away to be used later. Most of it was thrown away. The hides and fat were the important parts. Near the house great kettles were smoking over crackling fires. Into the hot kettles went the pieces of fat from the cattle. When the fat melted, it was put into cooling vats. After that it was poured into hides like bags, called *botas*. Five hundred pounds of tallow were worth about forty dollars. Another way to fix tallow was to make it into round blocks. A hole was made in the ground and a stick put in the middle. The melted tallow was poured into the hole. When the fat was hard, the block was pulled out. These blocks were easier to carry to the ship's boat. Some of the fat was saved for candles and soapmaking. The hides were soaked in salt water, stretched, and dried. Now the hides and tallow were ready to go to the ships. Bulky heaps of hides lay about. They were loaded into the *carretas*. A big ranchero like Juan Domínguez sent thousands of hides down to the harbor.

Rancheros were soon counting the loads with the ship's officers. The blocks or bags of tallow were weighed by the captain. He wrote the number down on a paper. Then the counting of the rough, folded hides began. The number of hides was written down. Two dollars was the usual price for each hide. Over the cliffs flew the hides like kites with broken strings. Men picked them up on the rocks below and put them on their heads. Then they loaded them on little boats to be taken to the ship. The tallow bags and sticks were carried down the slippery cliffs. It was hard work for the sailors and Indians who loaded. When all had been taken to the boats, the ranchero was given a paper. Now boxes were brought up the same cliffs where the tallow blocks had gone down. Perhaps the boxes had tea or silks from China. Maybe there were bright pieces of cloth or shoes from Boston. Rancheros, merchants, padres, and Indians—all wanted to trade for ship's goods. At last the boxes were loaded on the *carretas*. Such laughing and chattering as the loaded *carreta* creaked on the road toward home!

Over the cliffs to the rocks below
flew the hides to be loaded

Boxes of goods for trading were
brought up the cliffs

Even during this busy time there was time for play. Sometimes the ship stayed for several weeks or even months. The ship's crew and officers were welcomed in the ranchero's house. They danced and sang with the people in the pueblo. There were bullfights and barbecues and horse races! No wonder the trading ships liked to come to California! When they were gone, the sailors thought of the happy times they had there. They could not forget the gay, carefree people. They thought of the warm climate that made so many flowers and fruits grow. Wherever they went, they told about California!

Don Juan Domínguez used to watch the ships come and go at San Pedro. The time came when he could no longer see them. After he was blind, he went to live at Mission San Juan Capistrano. Before he went, he called an old friend to his house. "My friend," he said, "I want you to take care of Rancho San Pedro for me. As you know, I have no family. But keep this land so that my nephew, Cristóbal, will have it someday. When you are gone, it will be his rancho. Until then—you may stay here and use the land." His friend agreed to all he said.

But one day he forgot his promise to old Don Juan. He let a soldier use part of the land without telling Cristóbal. When Cristóbal heard about it, he was angry. Finally, the soldier, Juan Sepúlveda, went to Monterey to ask the governor about it. On the way back he stopped at Mission La Purísima. It was a day when unfriendly Indians made an attack on the mission. An Indian arrow struck and killed him. After that the governor sent word to Cristóbal about the rancho lands. The Sepúlveda children were given the part called Palos Verdes (Green Trees). The rest of the land would belong to the Domínguez family. They still had 38,000 acres left! Cristóbal's son, Manuel, took care of the rancho after that. He became *alcalde* in the pueblo, and his word was law.

The years after that were not the happiest ones at Rancho San Pedro. Once there was a battle fought on the rancho. That was about the time the Americans were trying to take the pueblo of Los Angeles. Then followed the gold-rush years, and many men left the rancho to go north. Later came the dry years—years when no rain fell. Many wild horses had to be driven over the cliff to save grass for the cattle. Cattle bawled and walked slowly across fields, looking for grass. There was no "run through the mustard" in those years. In wet years, the yellow mustard grew higher than a man's head. Then the cattle hid in it. The *vaqueros*, at full gallop, made a "run through the mustard." The cattle to be counted were driven out of hiding. But in the dry years, the mustard fields were only forests of dry stalks. Ranchos, large and small, were lost all over the state during those years. Rancheros borrowed and could not pay the money back. But the Domínguez family was one family that never lost its land. Today some of it is still owned by the same family.

The once charming home of the Domínguez family has been made into a school for young priests. In the chapel is a window with the words, "Domínguez, 1826." Oil wells cover the hills where part of the rancho used to be. The harbor of San Pedro has had many changes too. It took many years and millions of dollars to make a good harbor there. Now great ships come and go from all parts of the world. Hundreds of fishing boats bring fish to canneries and markets. At times there are many battleships anchored in the harbor. Along the shores are docks and warehouses. The Bay of Smokes has become one of the great harbors of the world!

JOSÉ MARÍA VERDUGO
WHO MEASURED HIS RANCHO ON HORSEBACK

José María Verdugo, another Spanish leather-jacket soldier, also became a ranchero. At first he was happy just to be a soldier at the San Diego presidio. When he became a soldier at Mission San Gabriel, he changed his mind. He saw great herds of cattle on the rich mission lands. "My soldier's pay is small. I think I will buy some cattle and sell hides to trading ships. Perhaps I will not always be a soldier anyway." So he bought a few cattle and used land not far away from the mission.

Some time later, Don José was married at the mission. Almost as soon as the bells stopped ringing, he began to make some plans. "How would you like to own some land?" he asked his new wife. "My friend, Juan Domínguez, has a rancho. He and I came to California together. It may be that Governor Fages will give me one too." "Where would you like it to be?" she asked Don José. "The place by the mountains where we met the first time," he said. "Yes—I am going to send a letter and ask for that land."

One day Don José's wife met him at the door. "Don José, there is a letter here from the governor. Do you think it is bad news?" she asked. "Let me open the letter quickly!" said Don José. "I think it will be good news. Let's see—the governor says, 'You may have the land!' What did I tell you? It is wonderful news. We will have our own rancho. Juan Domínguez has a rancho by the ocean. Now we will have one by the mountains! We were soldiers together and now we are rancheros!" "But, José," she said, "don't forget that you are still a soldier. How can you be a ranchero too?" "That is true. Well, let's see. I will let my brother take care of the rancho for a while. But someday you will see— we will be there too!"

A few years later, José Verdugo became ill. He sent word to the governor at Monterey.

"I find myself in poor health," the letter said. "May I leave the army and live on my rancho? I now have five girls and one small boy. With my brother and my family I will be happy to live at Rancho San Rafael." The governor gave his answer: "You may retire to your rancho. Remember not to let your cattle graze on mission land. And treat the Indians kindly!" Don José was glad to do what the governor said. Before long, he had twice as many cattle on his rancho. Many white sheep dotted the green hillsides, also.

One day Don José came into the house with a worried look. "Whose sheep are those grazing on our land?" he asked his brother. "Not only are there sheep, but ditches for water have been built. And huts for the shepherds as well. I do not like this!" His brother said, "The sheep probably belong to Mission San Gabriel. There is a new padre there. Perhaps he does not know where our land begins. Write to the governor and tell him that our land is being used." Don José did send word to the governor. The governor sent word to the mission: "The sheep belonging to the mission are to be taken away from Rancho San Rafael." Over on the other side of the rancho there was trouble too. No one seemed to know exactly where the line was on the Mission San Fernando side. Crops were harvested on the land that Don José thought belonged to him. This time the governor sent word to the *alcalde* in the pueblo: "Go out to Rancho San Rafael and help Don José María Verdugo. His land is between two missions. Measure his land so that all will know which land is his."

So Don José, the *alcalde,* and the *vaqueros* went out to measure the land. The *vaqueros* brought with them a fifty-*vara* (about fifty yards) reata. On each end of it was a long stick. Then the *vaqueros* measured the land with the leather reata. One of them held the long stick at the starting place. The other one galloped on his horse until the reata was straight. He put his stake or stick in the ground. Then the other *vaquero* galloped with the reata in the same manner. Thus the two measured mile after mile, fifty yards at a time. The *alcalde* and Don José made a map as they went along. Each corner was marked.

The rancho lands were all measured in this same way. Not all land was measured so carefully. The corners were not always well marked. Maybe a pile of stones was used.

The vaqueros measured the land with a rawhide reata

He owned the land as far as he could see

Later the pile of stones was gone. Perhaps a stream was used to mark one side. Later the stream became a dry creek. This kind of measuring caused trouble later for the owners. Sometimes they could not even prove that the land belonged to them. But Don José tried to mark his land well. He wanted the map to show exactly where his land should be.

Now Don José felt at peace with all around him. It was well that he did, for he was growing old. He made a will one day which said, "I leave Rancho San Rafael to my son, Julio, and my daughter, Catalina. I want them to keep it always and enjoy it."

Even after California became part of the United States, Rancho San Rafael was the same. No one worried. No one hurried. There was always plenty to eat. Fresh beef in

30

the pueblo sold for one cent a pound. "But who has to go to the pueblo for meat?" Don Julio said. "There is plenty of beef on our hills. Rope a steer—that's all there is to it. That doesn't cost even one cent a pound!" Julio had many sons to help him on the rancho. He found he had to build more houses, his family was so large. And the cattle herds grew larger and larger.

Nothing pleased Don Julio more than to ride into the pueblo of Los Angeles. Around his head he tied a black silk handkerchief. Over this was a low-crowned black hat with a wide brim. A strap under the chin held it on as he galloped in the winds. His jacket was of heavy black cloth or sometimes velvet. There were rows of gold buttons and fancy stitches on it. His trousers were split to the knees at the side. The edges had fancy stitches to match the coat. He looked exactly like a Spanish *caballero,* or gentleman. People could remember old Don José María Verdugo. "There goes old Don José's son, looking like his father!" they said.

All of the Verdugos were fine riders. Don Julio told his sons, "Don't ever forget that a Californian's home is the back of his horse! The man who cannot ride is only a half a man! I guess that is why we have no fish on our tables," he said with a twinkle in his eye. "Because we do not know how to fish from the back of a horse!"

Part of Rancho San Rafael was still wild country. Visitors wanted to come to the fiestas and rodeos at the rancho. But they were afraid of the bears that roamed every-where. Don Julio wanted visitors, so he had to do something about the bears. He sent *vaqueros* to meet the visitors who came up the Verdugo road. Guns were fired to scare the bears back into hiding! *Vaqueros* waved their bright serapes at them from a safe distance on horseback! "That is a dangerous trick!" the people said. But they rode on up the road safely.

Don José had left the rancho to his two children. Many years passed before they divided it. Catalina decided that she wanted the northern part. She remembered how beautiful it was with many oak trees. She could not see the land and trees any more, for she was blind. Julio took the southern part of the rancho for his share (now Eagle Rock

They made a map as they went along

and Glendale). But Don Julio lost his part of the rancho. Most of the adobe homes fell into ruins. One of his sons built a home for Catalina on her part of the rancho. This home is still standing today.

An adobe home which visitors may see today is owned by the city of Glendale. The Sanchez adobe stands in a little park there. The land on which it was built was given to María Sanchez by Catalina Verdugo. Those who visit it may see a home as it was in those early days. Each year in Glendale there is a fiesta called Verdugo Days. The old Rancho San Rafael may be forgotten, but the name of Verdugo is still remembered.

Those who visit the Sanchez adobe may see a home as it was in those early days

BERNARDO YORBA

AND WHAT HIS SONS LEARNED ABOUT REATAS

"Rancho Santa Ana was given to me by my father, José Antonio," Don Bernardo told his sons. "He came to California with Gaspar de Portolá and Father Serra. That was in 1769, long before rancho days. When my father left the Spanish army, he asked for some land. This rancho by the Santa Ana River is the land he wanted. I still remember what people used to say. They thought my father could ride fifty miles in a straight line without leaving his land! Those were good days, my sons. But we still have plenty of land—more than we can use."

By 1850, Don Bernardo Yorba was called the greatest ranchero of those days. His home was the biggest in the Santa Ana Valley. It had more than fifty rooms! All the way around the two-story house was a covered porch. Don Bernardo called it a *corredor*. In and about the *corredor* were storerooms and shops. Four Indian women were needed all the time just to comb wool. Others who sat near the kitchen door patted thin *tortillas* for hours. Indian men fixed hides to be used for saddles, harnesses, and reatas. Others worked with wool or silver. Oh, there were plenty of servants! Nearly a hundred of them—maybe more! They all lived in a little village not far away from the big house.

When cattle were needed, two men would lasso, throw, and kill them. Then the hides were skinned and stretched. The fat, melted into tallow, was put into bags. The best of the meat was used, either fresh or dried. The rest of it was left for dogs, bears, or coyotes. Some of the meat was made into dried beef, called *carne seca*. It was cut into strips an inch thick. The strips were left in salt water for several days. Then they were hung from trees. The sun dried the strips until they became hard, black, and dry. "It may not look very good," said good-natured Don Bernardo, "but it's good food just the same." All the *vaqueros* kept it in their saddlebags. On a journey, there was nothing like it to keep one from getting hungry.

One day Don Bernardo said to his best Indian *vaquero*, "The boys are learning to break horses. They must have good strong reatas of their own. I want you to show them how to make them." So the *vaquero* showed the boys how a reata was made right from the beginning.

The cowhide was fixed with great care. After the hide was well dried, the *vaquero* cut a round hole in the middle. Starting from the middle, he cut a strip around and around the hole. When he reached the outside of the hide, he had a strip about sixty feet long. Now he split the long strip into two strips. They were soaked in water until soft and ready to be stretched. The boys watched him tie one end of the strip to a strong, low limb of a tree. On a nearby tree he chose another branch. "Now you boys will have to help me," he said. They pulled the two limbs toward each other until the strip could be tied to the second branch. When the boys let go, the branches sprang apart and the wet strip was stretched straight and tight.

When the strips dried, they were as long as they could be stretched. Now they were taken from the tree limbs. A sharp knife was used to cut off the hair and smooth the leather strips. At last the *vaquero* was ready to braid the reata. Four strands were used. He tied the ends to a pole. "Isn't it too long to handle easily? How can you braid it when the strips are so long?" asked one of the boys. "You are right. It is better to start in the middle and do one end at a time. We'll braid one end and roll the rest into a ball until the first end is done," the *vaquero* said. "Now, we wet it first, then pull —braid—pull—braid. You see, I make it tight as I braid. Then it will be smooth as well as strong. As he finished one end, one boy asked another question: "What is that loop you have left at the end?" "The reata will slip through that smooth little loop," he answered. "And when you circle a loop around the feet of the cattle, you'll see why you have it!" When it was done, the boys agreed that it was a fine reata. "It will be used in many a corral and many a rodeo," they said. "More than that," said the reata-maker. "You and your children may use it to measure many more miles of Yorba lands!"

There always seemed to be visitors in the Yorba home, even though it was not near the pueblo. A visitor riding home from Los Angeles might meet someone on the way to the Yorbas'. "Yes, my friend," he would say, "I am to have dinner at the Yorbas' today. Dinner at the Yorbas' means butter and cheese. Few ranchos have that! But Don Bernardo has Indians who milk fifty cows a day! Won't you come along too? You will be just as welcome as I." They would trot along until they met another horseman. He, too, would be asked to go along. When they came to the Yorba door, there might be six more than the invited guest! No matter, all found a welcome there. And not only for dinner, but for the night as well. "You must stay for a *fandango* this evening," Don Bernardo would say. "Tomorrow we will ride out to see the herds. We have done nothing yet! But we have big plans! You shall see! Maybe we will have a horse race, for we usually do. Stay, my friends, there is always something to see—

Nothing was needed so much as a good reata—unless it was a good horse

Pull, braid, pull! That's the way to make a strong reata!

Down went the calf as the reata circled his legs

and always a good time!" And of course the visitors were glad to stay as long as they could.

Don Bernardo's daughter, Ramona, married a neighbor. He was an American, Don Benito Wilson. Don Bernardo gave his daughter many wedding presents. He gave her a chest of silk dresses. Each one had cost a hundred dollars! And there were satin shoes to match each dress. "Each of my daughters will get a chest of dresses such as this when she marries," he told Ramona. He had stored away many yards of the finest silks and satins bought from trading ships.

Tomás Yorba was the one in the family who really liked fine clothes. He liked to ride, but when he did, he wore fine satin jackets and trousers. On his feet were buckled shoes. His hat was trimmed with silver lace and braid. On feast days, he used his silver saddle, bridle, and spurs! "Yes, Don Tomás is the best-dressed man in California!" people said. "Probably his sons and their sons will wear the same clothes. Styles never change. He could wear his grandfather's clothes and still be in fashion."

Changes began to come after California became a part of the United States. One day everyone at the Raimundo Yorba house was excited! News came that a stagecoach was going to pass nearby the home. It was to carry people and mail from San Diego in the south to San Francisco in the north. "And it will go right by our door?" asked the Yorba children. "Not every trip, but once in a while it will come very close," their father explained. The first day it came, every man, woman, and child went down the bluff three miles away to see it go by. They waited a long time. At last they heard the rumble of the stagecoach. They heard the clatter of horses' hoofs down the road. Over the hill came the red coach drawn by six galloping horses. It swayed and bumped as it came! Finally, the wooden brakes screeched as the coach came to a stop. Passengers, grimy and tired, climbed out to visit with the Yorbas. "It has been a wild ride," they said. "We had to cling to our places as best we could." "Time to go again," said the driver as he got on the high seat in front. "Everyone on!" he shouted. A man climbed on the seat with the driver and laid his gun across his knees. "He is there to guard the people and the mail!" Don Raimundo told those who watched. "What fun to ride a stagecoach!" the children said. Their father only said, "It costs money. Money is scarce these days. Better that you go 'on horseback anyway. And it costs nothing!" But the Yorba children were not sure. The stagecoach seemed much more exciting to them.

The Raimundo Yorba adobe still stands on the top of a little hill. One of the very early California families lives there. The rooms of the home are full of reminders of those days. The first Yorba adobe in the Santa Ana Valley is gone. But in 1950 a bronze tablet was put at the place where the famous home used to be. Today there is another Bernardo Yorba. Like the other Yorbas before him, he is a rancher. He and his family live on a part of the land once given by the King of Spain to his great-great-grandfather.

Don Bernardo used to sit on his white horse and look over the Santa Ana Valley. In the distance were the homes of his children and of their children. He would say, "There are the lands and the houses of the Yorbas. There is plenty for them and besides!" Today, thousands and thousands of new homes have been built on the Yorba lands. And some of the Yorbas still have their homes there too!

On feast days he used his finest stirrups and spurs

ANTONIO LUGO
AND WHY HE BROUGHT A PIRATE TO LOS ANGELES

Clang! Clan-ng! Clan-n-ng! The sharp tones of the bells rang through the early morning air! Why did the bells at Mission San Antonio de Padua ring so loudly? The usual reason was that a child had been born near the mission. Before the day was over, everyone would know the news. "I hear the Lugos have another son," said one woman to another. "Yes, I have just seen him!" said the other. "They are to name him Antonio María."

Some of the first things that Antonio could remember at the mission were the horses. Mission San Antonio was famous for its gold-colored palomino horses. Antonio loved to see how silvery-white their manes looked in the sun! No wonder everyone liked to ride them in the fiesta parades. "To be a good rider, begin young," his father told him. So Antonio learned to ride almost as soon as he could walk. By the time he was four years old he could ride almost any gentle horse. As he grew older, he learned to bridle and ride even a wild horse. He had many hard falls, but he always wanted to learn more.

The lesson he never forgot was the trick of using a rawhide reata. "Let your loop fly there, boy!" shouted the *vaquero*. Swish! Swish! The reata flew through the air. Antonio did not have good luck at first. But soon he learned to coil a reata and throw it well. Down went the calf as the reata circled its hind leg. The *vaquero* had made a branding fire. Now the branding iron was heated in the coals until red. Antonio winced the first time he saw the curl of smoke from the burned hair! The reata loosened and the calf scrambled up. There was the brand on the hide! Someday he might brand cows on his own rancho, he thought.

Some time later, Don Antonio was given just the land he wanted. He had seen it one day as he was riding south from the pueblo of Los Angeles. The San Gabriel River was on one side; the Los Angeles River on the other. Soon a heavy green carpet of grass spread for miles on his land. No wonder the cattle grew fat at Rancho San Antonio! Soon Don Antonio had more cattle than he needed. By this time he had several sons. One day he said to his boys, "You are now young men. I have more cattle than I can count. It is time for you to have ranchos of your own. Then I will give you some of my cattle." The governor said that the three young Lugos could have Rancho San Bernardino. "Now drive some horses and cows from this rancho to yours," said Don Antonio. "If you have the same good luck, you also will have more cattle than you need. What will you do then?" he said laughingly.

The boys spent most of their days riding and caring for the cattle on their new rancho. Sometimes bears came to attack the cattle and sheep. If none came, the boys went on a bear hunt. The *vaqueros* went with them, for they liked the excitement! Up over the slopes went the sure-footed horses! Rocks slipped and rolled into the canyon with a clatter. Before long they found a brown bear digging worms among the rocks. "Let me use my reata this time," begged the youngest Lugo. "I promise not to miss a loop!"

*There was the brand on the hide—and
it would always be there!*

Almost at once his reata hissed through the air. Another reata swished out on the other side. The two loops fell around the bear's neck about the same time.

The real trick was to bring the bear back home. This was where the *vaquero* showed his skill. He rode ahead of the wild bear. Now and then he slowed down to tease him. The bear shook his head angrily and jumped forward. With a shout the *vaquero* sprang out of the way. Little by little a few feet were gained. Finally they came to the pueblo. The bear was put in the bull-and-bear pit. On Sunday the people in the pueblo had a real show. In the plaza was the angry bear. A strong reata was tied to his hind leg. The other end was tied to a bull's front leg. Then the fight between the two began. People at a safe distance shouted excitedly. The bull usually started out well, but the bear usually won.

Don Antonio had excitement of another kind. One day he received word to come north. The message said, "That pirate Bouchard is coming to the coast. Take some men and go to Santa Barbara. Your help will be needed!" So Don Antonio and some soldiers hurried north. Each evening Don Antonio's wife watched for his return. One evening just at sundown, she heard a jingle of spurs. Across the plaza she could see two men on one horse. Don Antonio jumped from the horse and pulled a young man off with him. "And who is this sailor you have with you, Don Antonio?" she asked in surprise. "He is a prisoner taken from the pirate ship. He says his name is Joseph Chapman." "If he is in trouble," and Doña Dolores, "we will help him." "What he wants right now is a good soft bed!" said Don Antonio with a smile. After Chapman had gone to bed, Don Antonio told her the story.

"Well, Doña Dolores," he said, "the pirate Bouchard landed north of Santa Barbara. His ships came to a little cove near there, El Refugio (The Refuge). That is where the Ortegas live, you know. A few hours before this, the Ortega family left. Bouchard was so angry that he burned the house. But we put up a good fight! The pirates ran for their ships. But we took three of the men prisoners. And how do you suppose we did it? With our reatas! Just like roping cattle—or bears—ah, that was fun! One of them was very strong. That is the one asleep in the next room." "But, Antonio, we should not have a pirate in our home!" said Doña Dolores. "I think he is not really a pirate," said Don Antonio. "When the Ortegas came back, one of the daughters seemed to like him. She begged her father not to let anyone harm him. She asked me to bring him to Los Angeles with me. And so I did, Doña Dolores. But do you know—he couldn't even ride a horse! I had to hold him on my horse all the way here!"

As days went by, Don Antonio was glad that he had brought Joseph Chapman to Los Angeles. He said that he wanted to work and help in any way he could. A church was being built by the plaza. Wooden beams were needed. Chapman said he would take Indians to get them in the mountains. "I have cut trees before," he told Don Antonio. "I know just where the trees will fall." The Indians who saw him do this thought it was magic. After that they called him El Diablo José (Devil Joe). Others called him just Don José. The logs were hauled down the mountains. First they were dragged on one side, then the other. They were smooth by the time they came to the plaza. Then they were cut into large beams. Day by day the beams were put into place. And Don José, the pirate, was the one who helped most to build the church!

Don Antonio and Joseph Chapman became good friends. Don José had shown that he was a good citizen. Not only did he help with the plaza church. Once he built a ship at San Gabriel. People came from all over the state to see it sail from the harbor. He also helped build a mill for grinding wheat into flour. All the Californians seemed to like him. Don Antonio thought it was time that his friend had a home of his own. Many shining eyes glanced at the tall Yankee! But he thought of the days when he was a pirate. He remembered the day he came to rob the Ortega home. Now he wanted to go back there. Maybe Señorita Ortega would marry him. So he and Don Antonio rode back to the Ortega rancho. To Don José, the señorita was more beautiful than ever. Guadelupe Ortega thought he was more handsome than she had remembered! A few days later their marriage plans were told. After the wedding, Chapman and his wife went south again. This time the bride rode on the same horse with him.

When eighty years old, Don Antonio still rode his horse. As he rode down the dusty streets of the pueblo, all the people knew him. "No other man in California rides quite like that," they said. "And look at that saddle. Have you heard? It cost two thousand dollars!" Some people wondered why he still carried his sword at his side. "Probably he remembers the old days when he was a Spanish soldier," others said.

The Lugos had come to California among the first. No wonder that Don Antonio remembered the old Spanish days. The Lugos had seen the strong adobe walls of the missions built. They had lived through the rancho days. They lived by the plaza when the American flag flew there for the first time. The Lugo doors, both in the country and in the pueblo, were open to all visitors. The Lugo hospitality was well known all over California. The house by the plaza had become famous. It was the center of social life in the pueblo. The first college in the pueblo was started in this house. It was the beginning of Loyola College.

Some of the Lugo family still live in the old country home, now in the city of Bell. The famous home by the plaza in Los Angeles is gone. When Antonio Lugo first came, there were only a few houses in the pueblo. Horses trotted through the narrow, dusty streets. Now trains leave from the large station near the plaza. Autos, buses, and even a helicopter carrying mail travel where Don Antonio once rode his horse so proudly.

44

THE OLD
SPANISH AND MEXICAN
RANCHOS
of Los Angeles County

PACIFIC OCEAN

1 Andres Pico
2 Verdugo
3 Doña Eulalia
4 Hugo Reid
5 Luis Arenas
6 Palomares
7 John Rowland
8 Pio Pico
9 Lugo
10 Bruno Avila
11 Antonio Avila
12 Nieto
13 Nieto
14 Juan Temple
15 Dominguez
16 Sepulveda
17 Abel Stearns

THE ÁVILA FAMILY
AND HOW THE PUEBLO OF LOS ANGELES BEGAN

The name of Ávila has always been famous in Los Angeles. "Did our father Cornelio remember the day the pueblo of Los Angeles was founded?" Bruno asked his older brother. Francisco Ávila smiled and said, "Oh no, Bruno, he came here two years after the first colonists. He used to say that he might as well have been here the day it began, though. He knew the story of its beginning so well."

The first people who came to Los Angeles were called *pobladores*. It was Felipe de Neve, the governor of Lower California, who started the little pueblo. He had read the report of Portolá and his party. It said, "We came to a valley with a beautiful river. Along the banks of the river were wild grapes. There was a large plain and good land for planting. The Yang-na Indians lived there. It is the best place we have seen for a mission." No mission ever was built, but something else happened there.

"Why not a pueblo in this place?" thought Felipe de Neve. "The King of Spain wants people to start towns in this new California." The Viceroy liked the idea. He knew that the King would like it too. So Felipe de Neve spent hours laying out plans for the King's pueblo in California. He thought of many things. First of all, the pueblo should be near the river. Next, he thought hills should be nearby. Indians could be seen from far off if they came to attack. The pueblo was to be a square, six miles each way from the center. A plaza was to be in the middle. The pueblo church, the jail, and the homes were to be around it. But these were only plans. Who would live in this new pueblo?

At last De Neve found some people in Mexico who said they would come. After a long, hard journey the eleven families came to Mission San Gabriel. There they rested for two weeks. Some of them went ahead to see where the pueblo would be. "This is the place," the soldiers told the men. "Tomorrow you will bring your families here."

"What! Bring our families to this dusty place?" they asked. "Won't we have to sleep on the ground?" "Yes," was the answer, "but it will not be long before you will have homes by a plaza." "But there is nothing here!" they said. "Oh yes—there is a mission not far away—and there are Indian villages too. Look out across the plains. Someday orchards will be there. There may be great herds of cattle. Ships can stop in the bay not far from here. It is a wonderful place! You will see—where this lonely spot is will be a big pueblo someday. It may be even bigger than a pueblo—it may be a city!"

It was early morning, the fourth of September, 1781. It was the day the people were going to their new home. Their coming was like a parade. Felipe de Neve came first on his horse, waving the flag of Spain. He wore a black hat with long, white feathers. His blue coat was trimmed with bright red satin. Then followed the soldiers in their leather uniforms. Gray-robed padres from the mission walked along behind. The forty-four men, women and children came next. Some rode on horses; some were in clumsy two-wheeled *carretas*. Last of all came the Indians, who drove the animals. Just as the sun was setting, they came to the new place. Then Felipe de Neve said, "At this place you will build your homes. You have had the courage to come to live in faraway California. See to it that you always have the same courage. The name of this place is Pueblo de Nuestra Señora La Reina de Los Angeles." At first the people used only the name El Pueblo (The Village). Later they called their pueblo Los Angeles (The Angels).

The next day the governor marked the place where the pueblo was to be. A small piece of land was given to each family. The land did not really belong to them. It belonged to Spain. "Here are the house lots. Outside the pueblo are the farm lots. The land is yours as long as you use it," the governor said. The families were also given animals and supplies. They promised to pay for these things in the next few years. They would pay in crops and cattle that they raised.

There they were—a few people with a few animals. What could they do for houses? The only trees were willows that grew by the river. So they made houses out of willow poles and grasses and mud. The Indians told them there was not much rain. If there had been, they could not have lived in such huts. As soon as they could, they built better houses. The Indians helped them make adobe bricks. A few miles from the pueblo they found some tar pits. The sticky, black tar bubbled and boiled. Around the edges were dried chunks of tar, or *brea*. These chunks were piled into *carretas* and taken to the pueblo. Up went the chunks to the top of the roof. The sun melted the tar until it covered the mud roof. Such a roof kept the house warm in winter and cool in summer.

People of the pueblo went to the river for water. But how could they get the water to the fields? Water had to be brought to the fields to grow crops. A large *zanja*, or ditch, was built. "Now we can take water to the fields," the men said. "But," said the women, "we still have to carry water to our homes in jars!" So the *Zanja Madre* (Mother Ditch) was brought through the pueblo. Those farther away from the *zanja* had to have water brought by Indian water carriers. One of the busiest men in the pueblo was the *zanjero*. He had to see that the *zanja* was clean. He had to repair any breaks in it.

The pueblo grew very slowly. The center of life was around the little plaza. The town house was used for meetings of the *ayuntamiento* (council). The council met to make laws for the pueblo. Some of the laws seemed very strange. If anyone wanted to have a party, he had to pay two dollars. If a young man wished to serenade a señorita, he had to have a license. If he did not get one, he was fined one dollar. One rule said, "Sweep in front of your house to the middle of the street. Another law said, "Hang a lantern in front of your house after dark." In that way there was no expense for lighting. Adobe houses never burned, so there were no fires. There was no need for policemen. Young men took turns in guarding. There were no schools for many years. The water came from the *zanja*. Because of all these things, it took little money to run the pueblo. The one who had the most power was the *alcalde*. As he went down the street he carried a gold-headed cane. People bowed and stood to one side as he passed.

By 1800 there were seventy families and thirty adobe buildings in the pueblo. The pueblo began to spread out just a little more. Farther out from the pueblo were large ranchos. One of the ranchos was given to one of Cornelio Ávila's sons. A horseman came riding one day into the pueblo. "I have news that will make you happy, Don Antonio!" he said. "You have been very good at catching horse thieves! Now you are to get your reward." "What—reward me?" he asked. "Yes—that is the news I have come to tell you. You have been given the right to use the land called Sausal Redondo." "You mean the land by the willows where there is water?" asked Don Antonio with surprise. "Ah— that is wonderful! I will make this land my rancho—the Rancho Sausal Redondo of Don Antonio Ávila!" So he became owner of a great rancho (now Inglewood). But the boundary lines of his rancho were not very clear.

One day another citizen moved in on the land close by. Soon he was building not only corrals for his horses but also a house. Don Antonio said nothing. Then one day one of his men came racing to tell him bad news. "Don Antonio, I have just come from the pueblo. I saw Don Ygnacio Machado signing a paper. He said that he had a right to this land. He is at the *alcalde's* office now!" "Then I must stop him," said Don Antonio. He told the *alcalde,* "This land is mine that Don Ygnacio has on the paper." "But, Don Antonio," said the *alcalde,* "your lines are not clear. How do I know?" Then Don Ygnacio spoke up: "For three years I have lived there. You did not stop me. I have even built ditches and planted a vineyard." "I only let you because I wanted to be good to you," replied Don Antonio. Then the *alcalde* decided that Don Ygnacio Machado could have a part of the land. He called it Rancho Aguaje de Centinela (Water of the Sentinel) because of the springs there.

Some years later, Don Ygnacio decided to live in the pueblo. Now Antonio Ávila saw has chance. He visited his brother who lived in Los Angeles. "Ygnacio Machado is looking for a house in the pueblo," he said. "Yes, but why should I care what he does?" asked his brother. "Trade with him!" said Don Antonio. "Oh no," said Don Bruno, "my house in the pueblo is worth more. Why should I give up my house there for his rancho?" "But, Bruno—for our family—once more it will all belong to the Avilas!" So Don Bruno said that he would make the trade. When it came time to sign the papers, Don Bruno said, "I have been thinking, Ygnacio. I think my house is worth more than your

48

rancho." "But what more can I give?" asked Don Ygnacio. "I have no more money and no more lands." "Well——" said Don Bruno slowly. "How about some barrels of brandy made from grapes of your vineyard?" So it was agreed. Don Ygnacio had to add two barrels of brandy to his rancho to get one small house in the pueblo!

Another Ávila son, Don Francisco, chose to live in the pueblo. "If I want to be on a rancho, I'll go see my brothers," he said. "As for me, I like to live in the center of things!" So he built his house on Olvera Street by the plaza. Don Francisco decided that his house would have the best of everything. For one thing, he used glass windows. The glass was brought all the way from Boston by ship. Satin curtains were hung from the many windows. Furniture came from other countries too. The Ávila house was different in another way. People called it the "house of revolution." This was because secret meetings were held there. Men met there to make plans for changing governors.

Many years later, Doña Encarnación Ávila was living alone in her house by the plaza.

Bruno Ávila traded his house in the pueblo for this house on a rancho

The Ávila home on Olvera Street still reminds us of those long ago times

She heard that American soldiers were coming to take Los Angeles. As she left her home she said to a young boy, "Stay here and don't let anyone come in!" After a few minutes he heard a band playing. "I'll just look out the door and see what is happening," he thought. Before he knew it, he had gone to the plaza. Behind him the door to the Ávila home was open.

Commodore Stockton and his soldiers marched toward the plaza. "Find a good place to stay," he told some of his men. Down one street and up another they went. Then they came to the Ávila house on Olvera Street. Strings of red peppers and white onions hung drying on the front porch. A blossoming vine trailed over the roof. But the most surprising thing was the glass in the windows! The door was open. Stockton's men looked in. "This is a fine house," they said. "This place has rugs on the floor! Look at those satin curtains, men. And such fancy furniture too! This is just the place for us to stay." So in they went and made themselves at home. Here they stayed for a number of days waiting for General John Frémont. At last they heard that he had made peace at Cahuenga Pass. After the American soldiers left, Doña Encarnación came back. She lived there many years, watching all the changes that came to the little pueblo.

Through the years, life was gay around the plaza, especially at holiday times. Christmas time was the most important time of all. It was not just a day but a long season. Plans were made many days before Christmas Day. And many weeks of merrymaking followed it. Perhaps one family made candles. Another made bright red and yellow paper flowers. Some worked on costumes for the Christmas plays. The spicy smell of little cakes filled the kitchens. Kettles steamed on hearths. There had to be enough for all! Not just for their families, but for relatives too. Many came in from the ranchos to celebrate the holidays. No one wanted to miss the Christmas Eve service in the plaza church. Down the aisle came the shepherds in a play about the shepherds who found the Christ child. There was the fierce devil who tried to keep the shepherds from going on their journey. The *pastores* moved from the church to homes around the plaza. Everyone knew the words of the play and loved to hear them over and over.

Olvera Street was an important street in those days. Now just part of it is left—the part by the plaza. It is interesting to find a little part of Los Angeles as it used to be. A zigzag line of bricks across the street shows where the *zanja* once ran. Most of the adobe homes have been torn down. But the Ávila house is still there to remind us of those days. The porch looks out on the little shops of Olvera Street. These quaint shops line the block-long street. You can smell *tortillas* and tamales cooking. In some shops you can see sweet-smelling candles made. They are made in the same way they used to be. People up and down the street sell shoes and toys, pottery and candies.

The best time of the year on the street is Christmas time. It is then that Olvera Street looks even gayer and brighter than in rancho days. People there still follow some of the old customs. All the shops and the Ávila house are decorated for the Christmas parade (*La Posada*). The *Posada* is a parade that tells the story of the Holy Family's journey. It tells how Mary tried to find shelter (*posada*) on Christmas Eve when Jesus was born. After the parade the children are ready for the *piñata*. It is a large decorated bag or jar hung by a rope in the center of the street. One by one each child is blindfolded. Each one tries to break the *piñata*. When one child does, gifts and candies fall out! Then the children shout and scramble to get them.

There is another Avila house left besides the one on Olvera Street. It is called Adobe de Aguaje de Centinela. It is on the rancho that was once traded for a house in the pueblo. The Centinela adobe was all alone when Los Angeles was a pueblo. Now it looks out over the city of Inglewood on one side and Los Angeles on the other. Where cattle grazed by the hundreds, there are homes by the thousands! New homes stand around the adobe house on all sides. Planes roar overhead on their way to a field that was once a cattle and sheep ranch. The Ávilas were very fond of horse racing. But they never guessed that their home would one day overlook one of the largest race tracks in the United States.

The rush of life in the city today is quite different from the once lazy days. Los Angeles was then only a sleepy little pueblo with a long name. Now it is one of America's great cities!

PIO PICO
THE GOVERNOR WHO LOST ALL HIS LAND

Land—and fame—that's what Pio Pico wanted! He would never stop until he had both! "My father did not leave me an acre of ground or a mule!" Pio Pico used to tell his friends. "What is more—I was born in a brush shelter, not even a house! That was at Mission San Gabriel. And I worked for the padres there for eight years."

The first real home Pio Pico could remember was in San Diego. How could he ever forget the happy days there by the old plaza? He had merry times with his neighbors—the Bandinis, the Carrillos, and the Estudillos. There were a few days when he had to go to school too. His uncle, Don Joaquín Carrillo, taught some of the boys to read and write. Pio learned enough arithmetic to run a little store. Sometimes Pio went to the pueblo of Los Angeles to buy. His brother, Andrés, decided to be a soldier. So he spent his days at the presidio in San Diego.

Pio Pico grew restless. He was a gay young man and wanted excitement. His sister in Los Angeles thought he should start a store there. "And why not?" he thought. "For one thing, there are more people there." His sister's husband, Don José Carrillo, had the finest house in the pueblo. Don José was well known all over the state. Important visitors came to his house almost every day. They came to feast and dance in his home. More than that, they came to make secret plans with him. He and his friends were always putting a governor in or out! "Just wait, Don Pio—your turn will come," said Don José. "We like to throw everybody out—forget the past—begin again!" But Pio only said, "Maybe someday, but first I will start my little store by the plaza."

Pio thought of his friends and relatives in San Diego. They thought of him and often wrote letters to him. One day his uncle, Joaquín, sent exciting news. The letter said, "My daughter, Josefa, is to be married. You are her favorite cousin. We want you to be here.

52

She is to marry Captain Henry Fitch, an American trader." "That is strange," thought Don Pio. "She is the one the governor wants to marry. Something must have happened." But he took out his best clothes and rode south to San Diego. When he got there, he found the governor had sent a letter. It said that Josefa and the captain could not be married. "Both must be citizens of Mexico," the message said. "Never fear," said Captain Fitch to Josefa, "I will become a citizen. It will take only a few days." "But you do not understand, Captain Fitch," said Don Pio. "It is the governor who must let you become a citizen. He will never let you do this. You see, he wishes to marry Josefa himself!"

Don Pio wanted very much to help his cousin, Josefa. He turned to Captain Fitch and asked, "Is your ship still in the harbor?" "Why, yes—yes, it is," he answered. "Then I have a plan," Don Pio whispered. That night when all were asleep, there was a quick knock on Josefa's door. There stood Pio Pico. "Hurry, Josefa! A horse is ready for you at the corral!" "But, Cousin Pio, I cannot go. My family would not like it," said Josefa. "Come, Josefa. Captain Fitch is waiting for you at the cove. The ship must sail with the tide. You will soon be on your way to South America. Then you can marry your captain." Quietly and quickly, Josefa put her things in a little bag. Pio was waiting for her close by her window. As she came out, he turned to see that no one was watching. Then he swung her into the saddle and she rode to the sea. "Thank you, Cousin Pio," she said as she left. "We will come back happy, and no one will say anything." But when they came back later, Captain Fitch was arrested. He was taken to the padre at Mission San Gabriel. "You must do something to right this wrong," said the padre. "You should not have taken away one of our California girls." After the captain had been a prisoner for several months, the padre forgave him. One thing more he asked him to do. "Give a bell to the plaza church in Los Angeles," he told him. Every time Don Pio heard the bell ring, he thought of the night ride to the sea. And the bell still rings in the plaza church to this day.

Not many years after this wedding, Don Pio had a wedding of his own. María Alvarado, niece of the governor, was his bride. The Carrillo house had seen many gay weddings. But this wedding was the gayest of them all! Pio Pico wore his finest black velvet suit. On his hands he wore huge gold rings. Across his vest were two heavy gold chains with two gold watches in his pockets! Of course the governor came dressed in a black suit with gold braid! No one—north or south—wanted to miss this wedding. And dancing and feasting lasted in the Carrillo home for over a week!

As time went on, the Pico brothers were given the largest rancho in the state. There were really two ranchos in one—Rancho Santa Margarita y Las Flores. The 133,000 acres had once belonged to Mission San Juan Capistrano. The rancho was so large that Don Pio and Don Andrés could ride all day without leaving their own land. One of Don Pio's wishes had come true. He had land—lots of it! "Now to be famous!" he thought.

Juan Bandini, the Picos, and the Carrillos did not like the Mexican governor in California. Victoria was a governor no one seemed to like. Soon people began to say, "Down with Victoria!" After he was put out, Pio Pico's friends wanted him to be the governor. "No," he told them, "I have only a few friends in the north. It is better that I wait." He waited for four years. Then his chance came to become governor. And he made Los Angeles the capital of the state.

About this time many other things began to happen. Americans were coming to California by the hundreds! This worried Pio Pico. "They might even try to take California," he told his friends. Mexico thought so too. A message came from Mexico to him saying, "Get more money as fast as you can! Soldiers must have food, uniforms, and guns. California cannot be held without many soldiers to fight." There was only one thing for Pio Pico to do. He had to get money for these things quickly! He had to get as much as he could. Selling land seemed the easiest way. So he sold missions and the mission lands.

There were thousands of acres of rich land in the San Fernando Valley. Andrés Pico had rented this land some years before. "Now we must sell the Ex-Mission San Fernando lands," they decided. The new owner paid $14,000 for the whole valley around the mission. Land that Don Pio could not sell, he gave away. He gave it to his family and friends. If the Americans were coming, he would see that his friends had land. If there

"Ranchita" was the place he loved to be

were enough Californians holding ranchos, maybe the Americans would stay out. Later everyone would have to prove that the land belonged to him. "Until then—take and give away all you can," he said to himself.

But Pio Pico could see that the good days would not last. "Will I still be governor if the Americans come?" he wondered. "Perhaps I had better leave California." He did not want to go. He was proud of California and he wanted to be governor. But he wrote, "Good-by, my friends. I am leaving you. I am leaving the country of my birth and family." Sadly, he left for San Juan Capistrano, where his sister lived. There he hid in her home. One night he heard Don Juan Bandini talking outside his window. "Do you know where Don Pio has gone?" he asked the friend with him. "No," was the answer, "but if I did, I would tell him to leave the country." That was enough for Pio Pico. He did not want to be taken prisoner. So the last Mexican governor of California fled to Lower California.

It was a year before Pio Pico knew what happened after he left. News traveled slowly. The first news said the Californians were winning. He decided to go back to California. When he did, he found the war had ended between Mexico and the United States. Even though Mexico had lost, he thought the people might still want him for governor. But a letter to him from Monterey said, "California will now have an American governor. Go to your large rancho and live in peace."

Instead, Pio Pico sold Rancho Santa Margarita y Las Flores near San Diego. "I cannot be governor, but I can be near my friends," he said. So he bought a small rancho near Los Angeles. El Ranchito (The Little Ranch) was nine thousand acres. That was a small rancho for Pio Pico! On it he built a large house with thirty-three rooms. He wanted it large enough to entertain all his friends. And many guests did come to his home. Travelers as well as friends were always welcome. People came for miles just to celebrate with him. Everyone knew of his hospitality. One party followed the next. He wanted all who came to be gay! They might stay as long as they liked. Nor was there any thought of pay. Instead, there was usually a plate of money in the bedroom. The traveler could

An old adobe of rancho days stands in Encino, near Mission San Fernando

take what he needed for his trip. If he needed a horse, there was one tied nearby.

Pico liked nothing better than horse racing. He had many fine race horses too. From an early age, he bet on horses and games of all kinds. He would take a chance on anything! There was a story that he sometimes took a mule to the races. On it were loaded bags of silver coins. He could use these in case he ran out of money in his pockets! Don Pio was not the only one who liked to make a bet. Many cattle—even ranchos—were won or lost this way. Whenever horsemen visited Ranchito there was sure to be fun. "Plunging horses! Flying heels! Dusty races!.Ah—there is nothing I like better," said Pio Pico.

Any game the Californians could play on horseback was fun. In one game, a coin or handkerchief was dropped. At once a bet was made on which rider could scoop it up on the first try. In another game, a live chicken was buried in the ground up to its head. The horseman started fifty yards away. At full gallop he leaned down and tried to pull the chicken out of the hole. Other riders showed their skill with a reata. They knew the señoritas were watching them do these tricks. Many of the games were not so gentle. One of them was "tailing the bull." It was not so easy to catch a bull by the tail and throw him on his back! But the young men seemed to enjoy doing that.

Andrés Pico did not live with his brother at Ranchito. He bought some of the Ex-Mission San Fernando land. He kept the finest horses and best cattle there. He thought his two-story house in the valley was as fine as Don Pio's house. But Pio Pico decided to build another building. He still had plenty of money from the sale of his rancho lands. The old Carrillo home where he was married had been taken down. On that place by the plaza, he built the Pico House. It was not only the largest building in the pueblo, but the finest hotel of that day.

"Don Pio is one of the sights of Los Angeles," wrote a visitor about that time. "He is over eighty years old now. He still likes his jewelry and his velvet cuffs and collar. He is still friendly and kind to everyone. No one was ever more courteous." But many things happened to make Don Pio sad. First, his brother, Andrés, died. Then he saw that times were changing. His money ran short. He had to borrow and he could not pay the money back. It was easy to cheat him because he spoke little English. The court ruled that he would have to give up all his lands. "I belong to another time," he said sadly. So he left Ranchito, the rancho he loved, and went to live in the pueblo.

The house at Ranchito (present-day Pico, near Whittier) is still left. It stands as a memory to his happy days there. Seventeen rooms of the large home are left. The rest were carried away by a flood from the San Gabriel River. You can still see the rooms where dances were held. The front rooms were used by Don Pio himself. In two of the rooms, the floors had boards, instead of adobe. There were no banks in those days. Perhaps Don Pio kept his money and rings under the floor. The rooms seem darker and smaller than ours today. There was little need of light in them. People went to bed early and were up at sunrise. Most of their time was spent outdoors. In the home can be seen some of the furniture that he used. Other things are there to show how he lived at Ranchito.

Near Mission San Fernando the fine two-story home of Andrés Pico may be seen. It is even more beautiful than in his time. The old Pico House looks out over the same little plaza in Los Angeles. Rancho Santa Margarita y Las Flores (in San Diego County) is still a large rancho. Today it is owned by the United States Navy and is used for a marine base. All these lands and places remind us of the Picos. One can only wonder how they owned so much. Pio Pico started out with no land at all. During his ninety-three years, he was able to get thousands of acres of land! He gave away even more than he owned. It is true he died a poor man. He even had to live in the house of a friend. Once he was governor of a great state. Land—and fame—that is what Don Pio wanted. And today he is remembered for both of them.

A rancho days kitchen may be seen at the Casa de Adobe in Los Angeles

HUGO REID

YANKEE TRADER AND HIS INDIAN WIFE AT RANCHO SANTA ANITA

Down went the rusty anchor into San Pedro Bay! "Boom!" went the cannon on the ship. Soon everyone would know a trading ship was in. News would spread like fire from rancho to rancho.

"Here is where we get a load of hides and tallow, señor!" said the captain. He was speaking to Hugo Reid, merchant on the trading ship. "There is more hide and tallow trade here than anywhere else along the coast," he said. "That storehouse over there on the hill is usually full. It belongs to Don Abel Stearns. He is the richest man in the pueblo. If only these rancheros had the hides and tallow ready when we come. Some keep saying 'Mañana' and then we have to wait. We could go back in a week if we found enough hides to fill our ship." "I may not want to go back that soon—what then?" asked Hugo Reid with a smile. "That is a strange thing for you to say, Hugo. Your uncle in Scotland taught you to be a merchant. Have you not done well in Mexico and other lands? Look at your fine clothes! This place will never satisfy you. You love adventure too well." "Tomorrow I shall go ashore and see," was his reply. He did like adventure. But why not adventure in this new land?

The early morning sun made streaks of gold across the water. Before the day was over the water would be full of little boats. Back and forth they would pass from shore to trading ship. Loaded *carretas* drawn by slow oxen would stir up clouds of yellow dust. Some of the people would be on horseback. Some would be walking. All of them would be excited and gay! Already a thin line of shoppers could be seen on the dusty road.

Sailors went ashore to count the hides and bags of tallow. Hugo Reid would leave the bargaining to others. No such business for him. He wanted to visit the pueblo of Los Angeles. Nearby was a horse nibbling grass. A rope hung loosely around his neck. Hugo

Reid took him as his own and galloped away. He chose the open fields leading to the town. Tumbleweeds rolled across his path with each gust of wind. How dry and bare the country looked! Rains had not yet come to turn the hills and fields to green. But he liked this wide-open country.

He came to the pueblo about noon. He tied the horse to a rail by the plaza and began to look around. Where was everybody? Probably taking their *siestas*, he thought. What a strange-looking place. It was not like any other he had ever seen! It was only a small pueblo. He did not see even one wooden house. How crooked the streets were! He certainly was not going to walk in those dusty streets! There were no sidewalks, so he could do nothing else. His keen blue eyes looked from side to side. He did not want to miss anything. There was something about the place that he liked. What was it? Perhaps it was the sunny day. Maybe it was because there were so many flowers. Blooming vines were in almost every yard. Then a friendly voice in front of a shop said, "Are you a stranger here, señor? Come and stay for the night—or many nights. You are welcome!" "Yes," said Reid, "I am a stranger. I would like to stay with you. Do you have other guests?" "Only one—an American like us," he replied. "His name is Abel Stearns and he has a store there by the plaza." "Oh, he is the one who owns the storehouse at the harbor. Yes indeed, he would be an interesting man to meet!"

Hugo Reid went into the house. He was surprised to find floors of hard earth. The boards of the ceiling were held together with leather strips. No nails could be seen. Well, this was different! Soon delicious smells from the kitchen made him think only of his hunger. Hot pink beans (*frijoles*) and thick stew were brought in. Then came stacks of thin, brown *tortillas*. He rolled his *tortilla* into a cone and scooped up the beans. Last came a bowl of golden oranges. As the two sat drinking coffee, Abel Stearns came into the room. The rich Don Abel and Hugo Reid had much to talk about. Both were merchants and both had traded in Mexico. Before the evening was over, they became warm friends.

A few days later the two friends met again. This time it was at the Old Mill near San

Gabriel. Once a week Father Sanchez from the mission had a picnic, or *merienda,* there. That was how the padre met his friends of the pueblo and from the ranchos. That was when he heard all the news of the week. By the side of the stream Indians were busy cooking. A hot fire burned low in a pit in the ground. Large pieces of meat on sticks turned round and round over the hot coals. Juice and grease from the meat fell into the fire and made a sputtering noise. Could anything smell so good? A huge pot of beans bubbled over another pit. Hugo Reid unwrapped a tamale from a cornhusk. He was sure he had never tasted better food!

After one short week, Reid's stay came to an end. The trading ship was ready to sail, so he had to leave. He looked back at the yellow cliffs of San Pedro. He would not forget this land of sun, flowers, and friendly people. He would remember the music, the dancing, and the food. He would come back again as soon as he could. Two years later he did come back. He and a friend opened a store by the plaza. Some people came to see what he had.

One who came to his store was Doña Eulalia. For many years she had been housekeeper for the padres at Mission San Gabriel. Now she lived on her own rancho near the mission. It was given to her for her work at the mission. "I will take that silk shawl with the flowers," she said. "And those dishes—I would like those!" "Anything more, señora?" asked Hugo Reid. "No, I have more than I can carry now." "Then I will help you," he said. "You don't come into the pueblo often, do you?" he asked. "Often enough—for I like San Gabriel." "I like it too," he agreed. "Oh—you have been there?" "Yes, I was there when Father Sanchez was there." "Too bad. Now he is gone. San Gabriel is not what it was. You have not seen it lately? Then you must come. Put my bundles over there in the *carreta.*" Hugo Reid was surprised at what he saw. "I know," said Doña Eulalia. "You expected to see an Indian boy driving the oxen. Instead, you see a beautiful Indian woman. Victoria is beautiful. Anyone can see that!" Then she added, "Come for tea sometime, señor." "I will—and soon," he said.

He did go to San Gabriel. He remembered his first visit there. How changed and lonely the mission looked now. Some of the buildings had no roofs. Doors were closed,

Indians carried the heavy blocks of
tallow to trading ships

Adobe bricks by the hundred dried
in the sun

and no one seemed to be there. Then he went to Doña Eulalia's home. Victoria met him at the door. "*Buenos días,* señor," she said. "Doña Eulalia is having her *siesta* now." "Then I will talk to you," he replied. He told her that he had come from Scotland. "Then I wanted to see the world. And I have been traveling ever since, Victoria. I should like to hear about you." "There is very little to tell," was her answer. "My father was a great Indian chief. Many years I helped Doña Eulalia at the mission. I have been very busy. My husband and I have three children." Hugo Reid had not expected to hear this. He was sorry he had made the visit. His friends in the pueblo told him to forget the Indian girl. They urged him to go back to Mexico. "I like the country, the climate, the people," he said. "But if I cannot have Victoria, I might as well go!"

So he left the California he loved. A year later he heard from his friend, Abel Stearns. The letter said that Victoria's husband had died. Hugo Reid returned to California. And a year later, Victoria became his wife. Doña Eulalia saw to it that Victoria had a fine wedding. Indian women spent days cooking food for a feast. There was merry-making in San Gabriel for a whole week!

Not only did Hugo Reid get a wife, but also her lands. Victoria owned a small place near San Gabriel. Thorny gooseberries grew there, and so they called it Uva Espina (Gooseberry). He no longer cared to have a store in the pueblo. He had to spend his time showing Indians how to build the house. Adobe bricks by the hundreds dried in the sun. When the house was finished, Victoria would not move in. This house had two stories, and she would not live upstairs. She remembered earthquakes at San Gabriel. Once the towers of the mission had fallen down. Finally she agreed to live downstairs.

After a time Hugo Reid grew restless. Many of his friends had been given large ranchos. He decided that he, too, wanted a large rancho. But where? Not far from the mission was an oak-covered valley. Tall, blue mountains were to the north. There were silvery streams and fertile lands in the valley. "Here is the most beautiful place in the world," he said. "I will make it my home." He was not sure he would be given the land, for others had asked for it too. But in time Victoria was given the grant, "for the many services she gave to the mission."

Victoria's children loved the new home, which they called Santa Anita. Most of all they liked the little lake. Steps led down from the door to the boat landing. Sometimes they went for rides in a little white boat. Other times they spent watching the fish flash back and forth. Birds made nests in the tule grasses. Don Hugo bustled from morning to night giving orders. Indians planted fruit trees and grapevines. Seeds were sown for vegetables and grain. Uva Espina in San Gabriel was almost forgotten.

A runner hurried back and forth between rancho and pueblo. Don Hugo needed so many things for his rancho home. Then, too, he kept the records for Don Abel's store. One day the runner to the store took a surprise letter out of the pocket of his saddle. It was a letter asking Don Abel and Doña Arcadia to come to dinner at Santa Anita. Should they go? What would they find? Some people imagined Don Hugo living in an Indian grass hut. What Don Abel and Doña Arcadia found was quite different! After that other friends in the pueblo came to visit at Rancho Santa Anita.

Don Hugo now seemed to have everything. But again he became restless. Exciting days in other countries left pictures in his mind. Ranch life seemed too peaceful and quiet. He wanted to go to sea again. So one day Don Hugo sailed away. Back and forth he went from one country to another. Lonely months went by for Victoria at the rancho. When he came back he brought the finest shawls, laces, and silks to her.

One day Don Abel received a letter from him. It said, "I find I must sell either my rancho or Uva Espina. I cannot keep both places. Which one shall I keep?" Don Abel found it hard to give an answer. Finally he wrote, "Perhaps you should not be a ranchero any longer." So Don Hugo decided to sell the beautiful Rancho Santa Anita. A friend was glad to buy it for twenty-three cents an acre. No one would give him any more. Hugo Reid's life as a ranchero was over.

Now Hugo thought he would go back to sea. He would travel until he wanted no more. Just then he heard surprising news. Gold had been found in the north. "There would be adventure," he said. So he went to Sutter's Mill to try his luck.

Don Hugo came back from the north unhappy. The gold fields had given him no gold. He was forty years old, but his hair was silvery-white. "Old Reid," people called him now. Once again he and Victoria lived at Uva Espina. Their thoughts were of other days. No golden fields spread out before their door. No orchards hung heavy with fruit. No cattle dotted the wide fields. Only gay and prickly gooseberries grew in the small garden. Time passed slowly for Don Hugo. Then he remembered an old promise to Victoria. "Someday I will tell the people of California about the Indians," he had said. "They do not understand your people."

He thought no more of sailing to far places. He wrote of the life and language of the California Indians. Victoria helped him. She went back in her memory and told him of the early years. The Los Angeles *Star* was the newspaper in the pueblo. It was glad to print Don Hugo's twenty-two letters. Soon after writing them, Don Hugo died. For three more years, Victoria lived at Uva Espina. She soon lost everything. Even then she was proud and cheerful. Then one day she was buried by the mission where she had lived so many years.

The home at Rancho Santa Anita passed from one person to another. One day a man named Lucky Baldwin came. Under his arm he had a tin box heavy with money made from mining. Once he had seen this rich valley. He had not forgotten the wide acres of oak trees. Now he had plenty of money and wanted to buy the rancho. Two hundred thousand dollars was the price he paid. Instead of cattle, he bought fine horses. Racing stables were built. Around the Hugo Reid adobe he planted palms and willow trees. Visitors came to the little lake for boating. A fancy white house was built close by. Peacocks with golden and green feathers strutted here and there. Lucky Baldwin sold many of the acres. But the part by the lake where Don Hugo lived he kept for himself.

Now all may see this part of the old rancho. It is owned by Los Angeles County and the State of California. A garden of California trees, shrubs, and flowers has been planted

66

there. The adobe home of Victoria and Hugo Reid appears as it did in other years. Birds still build nests in the tule grasses. Peacocks roost in trees and wander proudly over lawns of homes nearby. Not far away are the racing stables of the race track at Santa Anita. They are much larger than any dreamed of by Lucky Baldwin. The lands around the old homes are even more beautiful than when Don Hugo Reid and his Indian wife lived there.

Hugo Reid's adobe stands by the little lake

DON YGNACIO PALOMARES
WHOSE RODEOS WERE SO EXCITING

The one thing that Ygnacio had always wanted was land. How wonderful it would be to have a strong house too. In it would be a fine family. Around him would be his friends to visit him. He wanted to be "master" of his house!

Ygnacio had a very good friend, Ricardo Véjar. For years they had shared land with a widow. This was on the Rancho de las Aguas (now Beverly Hills). One day the widow sent word to Don Ygnacio: "You and your friend will have to find other land. There is not room enough here for all our cattle." Something had to be done. Now was the time for Don Ygnacio to get his own land.

Ygnacio remembered a beautiful valley near the mountains. It was about a day's horseback ride east of the pueblo. Behind the valley was a mountain, white-tipped with snow in winter, bald in summer. Some said it was named Mount San Antonio for old Don Antonio Lugo. Others called it, as he did, Old Baldy. He had heard that Indians lived nearby. Maybe that was why no one had taken this San Gabriel Mission land before. No matter, Ygnacio would make friends with the Indians. They probably knew how to work on a rancho.

That summer the *alcalde* rode out with the two men. He went to help them measure the land. "Can you think of a finer place to live?" Ygnacio asked the *alcalde*. "Yes, in the pueblo," was his answer. "But, señor, is this not good land?" "Yes, it is and you may get rich, Ygnacio. As for me, I would rather not take a chance." "Chance—what do you mean?" "Well—there are the Indians, you know. You are many miles from the mission. You are as many miles from the pueblo. These Indians near here are from the mission and are friendly. But the ones in the mountains rob, steal, and kill!" "Oh, Ygnacio," said Ricardo, "maybe we'd better not come!" "No!" said Ygnacio firmly.

"We will come. We will not be scared!" "Then," said the *alcalde*, "let us measure the land. Each night I will think of you and hope you are safe."

Not long after that a paper was sent to the governor in Monterey. The paper said, "We have cattle and need a place for them. We would like a place known by the name San José. It belongs to no one now; once it belonged to Mission San Gabriel." Ygnacio Palomares signed his name at the end. Ricardo Véjar could only make a mark (X). The governor sent the paper to the *alcalde* in Los Angeles. On it the governor had written. "If you also agrèe, these men can have the land." The *alcalde* wrote, "Let the grant be given. The land has been measured, and the record put in a book." That was the way the two friends were given Rancho San José. All the rancheros were given land in much the same way.

The vaqueros herded the cattle into the corral

Don Ygnacio's house had not been built long when he was wakened one morning. "Don Ygnacio! Wake up!" called his wife. "Listen! Something is wrong. Hear the horses neighing—hear the noise of the cattle!" Just then a *vaquero* rode up, shouting, "Ygnacio! Indians!" Then Ygnacio saw that the bean field was on fire. After the Indians were gone, he saw what had happened. Crops were lost—buildings burned down around the house, horses stolen. But Ygnacio would not leave. "This is where I want to live," he said.

There were many happy times at Rancho San José. The families were always having dances, picnics, fiestas. They even made picnics out of washday. Clothes to be washed were saved for weeks. There had to be enough clothes to last from one wash to the next. The washing was done in the nearest stream. Flat rocks were there on which to pound clothes to make them clean. Clothes were piled into the *carreta*. Children thought it fun to bounce up and down on the piles of clothes! After the washing was hung on the bushes to dry, they ate lunch. Then came a *siesta* under the trees. In the evening, the men rode over to the stream to join the party. Then they all went home together. The children went to sleep by the piles of clean clothes. The rest laughed and sang as they rode back to the rancho house again.

The most exciting thing that happened at the rancho was the rodeo. In early California every rancho had a roundup or rodeo once a year. It was usually held in April or early summer. Sometimes there was another one in the fall. Because the ranchos had no fences, the cattle grazed together. At least once a year the cattle had to be separated and counted. Each ranchero had two brands. One brand (*fierro*) showed he was the owner. The other was a brand (*venta*) used when he sold the animal. The brand was burned into the side of the cattle. All brands were listed in a book of records. Sometimes the cattle were marked by cutting their ears in a certain way. When the cattle were crowded together, the earmarks could be seen more easily. There was a fine of nine dollars if a ranchero took cattle that were not his. That was a lot of money in those days. No one wanted to pay such a fine.

One morning Don Ygnacio heard the sound of a horse hurrying down the road. "I have come from the pueblo," said the rider. "It is rodeo time again. The *alcalde* beat the drums yesterday to tell the pueblo. Now I have come to tell you that one of the rodeos will be at Rancho San José next week. I must hurry on to tell the other rancheros to come."

This news pleased Don Ygnacio, for he enjoyed the thrill of roundup time. What Californian did not enjoy the excitement and fun of it? It was not so much the work as the play that went with it! *Vaqueros* spent days bringing the cattle to the rancho. This was not easy, because the cattle ran wild over the land. A large corral or pen was built. It was made of strong posts set close together. Don Ygnacio and Don Ricardo made careful plans. It was decided that Ygnacio would be *juez de campo* (judge of the plains). He would settle any questions or quarrels.

The rodeo sometimes lasted a week or more. Brush shelters were put up by the stream for the men and boys. Boards for tables were put in place under the trees. Pits were dug where meat was to be cooked. Fine young cattle were killed for the barbecue. Vegetables were brought from the garden. For days women patted and stacked the thin *tortillas*. A large brush *enramada* (shelter) for dancing was built. The younger girls made bright paper flowers to make the *enramada* look gay.

At last the first day of the rodeo came. Rancheros and their families came from miles around. Don Ygnacio was up early and on his favorite black horse. It was not long before he gave the signal for the *vaqueros* to bring in the cattle. What a noise there was then! Clouds of dust filled the air! *Vaqueros* yelled as they rode through the cattle and drove them into the corral. Their horses had been well trained to do this work. The cattle bawled angrily and tried to get away. Around the sides of the corral, women and girls watched. The men were proud to show the visitors how well they could ride and use the reata.

The cattle that had been branded before were counted and separated. One *vaquero* from each rancho kept the count on a stick. He cut a notch for every ten counted. The

71

What would the rancho do without a carreta?

baby calves followed their mothers. Then the *vaqueros* caught the new calves and branded them with the same brand. There were puffs of dust as riders dashed after runaway calves! The *vaquero* sent his reata into the air and made a neat catch! Then he tied the hind legs of the calf to one front leg! The branding iron had been heating over a fire at one end of the corral. Now the iron was pressed against the animal's left hip. A ribbon of smoke rose from the burned hair. The reata was pulled loose and the calf got to its feet. There was the brand—and it would always be there! After that the ranchero would know that he was the owner. For another year the branded cattle could roam over the pasture lands. Stray calves were given to the ranchero where the rodeo was held. Horses were not branded unless they were fine saddle horses. But cattle—that was different. The hides brought money or goods when it came time for trading.

The vaquero cut a notch for every ten counted

When the work for the day was over, the time for fun began. While the men rested, food was put on long tables. Never had food tasted so good! After supper there was a great rushing about. Boots were dusted. Girls put on their best ruffled skirts and bright sashes. Outside, the moon helped to light up the dancing *enramada*. Soon gay music set the feet and hearts to dancing. It seemed easy for Californians to work all day and dance most of the night! The rodeo was a time of work, but it was also a time of fun.

In later years Don Ygnacio built another house by the side of the San Bernardino road. It was the road that led from that place to the pueblo of Los Angeles. All the people who came along the road passed his door. Under the pepper trees tired travelers found welcome shade and cool water. "There is another thing that will make people stop here," he told his wife. "I'll have a little store at one end of the house. Then I can talk to people who buy. I will get all the news without leaving my rancho." Day after day, covered wagons came from the East. Where were they going? To the West—always to the West, looking for land or gold. Whether the travelers bought or not, Ygnacio never let them go hungry. He even took them into the house for a night's rest. To all he said, "This is your house. Welcome!"

Some of the new rancheros in the valley planted orchards. Don Ygnacio did not wish to do that. The orange trees he had brought from Mission San Gabriel were doing well. In his front yard he had a few lime trees. Huge bunches of green grapes hung under the broad leaves of the vines. "Enough for ourselves but no more," he told his family. "Cattle will always make us rich. Cattle are not much work to keep. Cattle need only be branded. Why should we plant orchards and work hard?"

When the dry years came and cattle died, Don Ygnacio was not sure he had been right. Even then he tried to be patient. Don Ricardo Véjar had a harder time. He had become a rich man. He had a larger home than Don Ygnacio. His herds were larger too. Now he found he had to borrow money. Ygnacio warned him, but he made a mark on a paper. When the time came to repay, he had little money. He had to give up most of his part of Rancho San José.

One family after another came to live in the house of Don Ygnacio. Many changes were made in it. Once the home had been the center of the rancho. Now it became just a house in the country. It was alone and empty for a long time. Rains washed away the adobe bricks from part of the house. Now the State of California owns it. Once more the adobe walls are as strong as when Don Ygnacio built them. The same kinds of flowers and fruit grow in the garden. Twice a week visitors are shown through the house. Some of the furniture came from the Véjar family. Some came from other California homes. In the little store are old record books. In one room are the saddles, spurs, and branding irons of Don Ygnacio. To all who come, the old adobe still offers a welcome. Its plain rooms and quiet garden still tell of the early California family.

Today those who live there have made of the Pomona Valley an orchard and a garden. Every year there is a big fair. People show with pride their horses, cattle, fruits, and flowers. Many of those who could remember the old days are gone. But some of the Palomares, Véjars, and members of other early-day families still live in the valley. Once a year a special program is given with Spanish songs, dances, and games. In this way the people of today can see some of the things that were done in gay rancho days.

To all who come, the old adobe still offers a welcome

SANTA BARBARA
WHERE FIESTAS WERE ALWAYS FUN

It was the year 1782. Captain José Francisco Ortega's party marched up the coast. With the party was Father Serra and Governor Felipe de Neve of Lower California. The new Mission San Buenaventura had just been founded. Father Serra wanted to found a mission at Santa Barbara. "That will have to wait for a while," said Governor Neve. "We must have places for our soldiers to live. These Indians at Santa Barbara are friendly. Others may come who are not friendly. We cannot build two buildings now. The presidio must be built first." Father Serra was disappointed. But he held a service that began the presidio. He made a record of all that happened that day. This record may still be seen at Mission Santa Barbara. Father Lasuén came to found the mission four years later.

Captain José Francisco Ortega became the first *comandante* of the presidio. One day he told his men, "Supply ships may not always come from Mexico. We must have enough food to take care of ourselves. We need storehouses full of grain. To grow crops we must have water." So a ditch was dug from a nearby stream. Grain, vegetables, and fruit trees were planted. Sometimes the soldiers thought they had become farmers instead of soldiers. But they always had enough to eat. They felt safe behind the strong adobe walls of the presidio.

Captain Ortega was given Rancho El Refugio up the coast north of Santa Barbara. At that time only Spanish ships could trade with Californians. These ships stopped in the wide crescent bay at Santa Barbara. But ships of other countries knew about a little secret cove at Rancho El Refugio. Trade was carried on here with the Ortegas and other rancheros. One day the Ortegas heard that another kind of ship was coming there. A sea captain brought the news that the ship of Bouchard, the pirate, was coming to El

75

Each year in August, Santa Barbara has a gay fiesta

*During "Old Spanish Days" men in Spanish costumes ride on
beautiful horses*

Refugio. Quickly they packed what they had and hurried inland. When Bouchard and his men came, they found only an empty house. Bouchard was angry, so he burned it. Soldiers and friendly rancheros hurried to the rancho to help. They drove off the pirates and captured a few men. One was Joseph Chapman, who later married an Ortega daughter.

Another famous *comandante* at the presidio was Don Raimundo Carrillo. He became founder of a well-known family in California. He had seven sons but only one daughter. The man Doña María married later became *comandante* of the presidio. He was Don José de la Guerra y Noriega.

Everyone in Santa Barbara and the whole state knew the De la Guerras. The story of Santa Barbara is almost the story of that family. The name is still well known today. Doña María Carrillo de la Guerra was almost as famous as her husband. There were always guests in their fine home. Governors always stopped there. So did other important men in the government. Whoever came was made welcome.

Don José de la Guerra was a very serious man. He was a good friend of the padres at the mission. He was one of the richest Spanish Californians. But he was always ready to lend money to his friends. He wanted all the people of Santa Barbara to be friendly and courteous. More than anything, he wished them to have fine manners. And the people did become well known for their manners and hospitality. Visitors noticed all these things. "It is because of Don José de la Guerra!" they said.

Don José had ranchos near Santa Barbara. But he liked to live in the presidio town. "Let the *mayordomos* take care of the ranchos," he said. "As for me, I would rather be in my Santa Barbara home. There I can see my friends who come to visit from everywhere." Other Santa Barbara rancheros liked this idea. They, too, owned ranchos but liked to live in Santa Barbara most of the year.

These people in Santa Barbara were a happy people. They did not have to work hard. There were enough Indians to help with the work. That meant there was time for fun and play. Someone would say, "A fiesta—let's have a fiesta tomorrow!" At once everyone scurried about getting ready. Or perhaps a trading ship was in the harbor. "Have you seen? A trader is in! Time for a fiesta!" Then the men from the ship came to join in the fun! When visitors or relatives came there was a fiesta. Perhaps just a family had one. Fiestas on the rancho were even gayer than in the pueblo. Perhaps fifty or more neighbors were invited. For days the Indians helped the Doña get food ready. There didn't have to be a real reason for a fiesta. People had them anyway. They liked merrymaking at any time! Pleasure came first and work second in those days!

Fiestas were held on special feast days. They began with a service in the church. Sometimes there was a parade. Young men in gay clothes rode on their finest horses. The best silver-trimmed saddles to be had were used. Always there was a feasting at noon. In the afternoon there were horse racing and other sports in the plaza. Of course music and dancing were part of every fiesta. But even gay fiestas had to come to an end. The clanging of the mission bells told them it was time to go home. The young people galloped home on their fine horses. Tired children and older people rode in the *carretas*. All laughed and talked of the happy time they had just had together.

More and more trading ships came to Santa Barbara. Many of the traders stayed. These newcomers did not try to change the presidio town. "We like it just as it is," they agreed. One by one, the De la Guerra daughters married Americans. One daughter, Anita, married an important trader, Alfred Robinson. Their wedding was one that is still remembered in Santa Barbara. A famous writer once told the story of the wedding like this: "The ship's cooks came ashore. For three days they made cakes for the wedding. Everyone in the town was busy with plans. The De la Guerras were the busiest of all. A large tent was placed in the patio where a feast was to be spread. At last the wedding day came. The doors of the mission church opened wide. Out stepped the beautiful bride all in white. Clouds of smoke rose from the cannons on ships at anchor. Flags of many colors were sent flying from the mast. Then the sailors headed for the shore. They, too, were invited to a *fandango* at the De la Guerra home. Everyone came whether invited or not. They came in the finest and brightest clothes they had! Almost all of Santa

Each spring about five hundred ride from rancho to rancho

Barbara was there. In the patio were Spanish and American dances. Inside the house, friends of the bride danced the graceful *contradanza*. It was the richest and finest wedding ever held in California." Each year during fiesta, the story of this wedding is told again.

One day the padre asked Don Alfredo Robinson, as they now called him, "When will your country come and take California?" Even he did not think it would be soon. Late in the year 1846, word came that General Frémont was marching south. Spanish Californians decided that they would fight. "We will not let those Americans take California if we can help it!" they said. So they made a plan. They knew Frémont would have to go through Gaviota Pass. "We will hide where the pass is steep and narrow," they agreed. "His soldiers will not get any farther than that! We will roll the biggest rocks on them. That will be the last of them!" But the plan did not work that way. This was because of Don Julian Foxen, who had a rancho near the pass.

At the end of a very hard day, Frémont's men stopped to make camp. They were hungry and their clothes were wet and heavy. Soon a fire warmed them and dried their clothes. Then, they saw a little light in a house not far away. "Go find out who lives there," said Frémont. They went and soon came back with meat and flour. With them came a tall ranchero, Don Julian Foxen. Don Julian knew of the Californians waiting at Gaviota Pass. He decided to tell Frémont about them. What good would killing these few Americans do, anyway? he thought. So he told Frémont and promised to lead the soldiers over another pass. "Few know the way over San Marcos Pass—but I do!" he said. It was Christmas, but the men thought little of that. A cold rain poured all day. They had to cut a path for themselves. Two days later the tired soldiers marched into Santa Barbara. It was Sunday, and most people were in church. No town was more quietly taken. The Californians still waited at Gaviota Pass. Frémont and his men marched on south. At the presidio the American flag was left flying in the ocean breeze.

It did not seem to matter who held California. "We will do as we always have. The old ways are still good!" the people of Santa Barbara said. But they did begin to think more about having schools. Before, they had thought boys should be good horsemen. They should have good manners and be gay. Girls should embroider nicely and dance well. Did they need schools for these? Anyway, there were very few books. But when the Americans came, the first real school was started in the old presidio. Other changes had to be made too. There was a new council. Don José's son became the first mayor. The new council needed money. City lots were sold to run the city government. Some of the lots sold for one dollar each!

The years of the gold rush came. Word about Sutter's gold did not seem to interest those in Santa Barbara. Not many men left for the gold fields. Life was happy as it was. What need was there for gold? Travelers by the hundreds passed through the town. Most of them were from Mexico. Many camped at the old presidio. Old Spanish songs floated through the night air as bonfires burned. Then the gold-seekers hurried on their way. Some of the rancheros drove cattle north. Prices were high. They soon became rich. What was to be done with the money? They bought saddles made with silver and spurs trimmed in gold. Señoras and señoritas had finer silk skirts. They had brighter shawls, lacy *mantillas,* and more beautiful high combs. Men had gayer velvet jackets and sashes of all colors. Better furniture was bought for the houses. People were richer without having to go to the gold fields.

Santa Barbara is much larger than it was in rancho days. But Santa Barbara still likes to remember those days. The love of parades and fiestas has lasted through the years. When the moon is full each August, Santa Barbara has a fiesta. It is called "Old Spanish Days." For three days there are parades and plays, costumes and music. Just as of old, the fiesta begins at the mission. On the steps of Mission Santa Barbara there is a play. It tells the story of the presidio and the mission. When the story is ended, fireworks light up the mission gardens. The second day there is a parade. You can see men and women in Spanish costumes on golden-colored palomino horses. Some of the silver-trimmed saddles were made in rancho days! There, too, are old *carretas* and stagecoaches. In the Plaza de la Guerra is a market like the Spaniards had. In the courthouse gardens are singers and dancers. Many belong to early California families. People are friendly as they were in rancho days.

Old books are brought from Mission Santa Barbara for the fiesta. There you can see the careful writing of Father Serra. There is an order written by Don José de la Guerra. It tells the padres to hide their treasures because of the coming of the pirates. There are many old rancho-day letters. One by Don Alfredo Robinson tells how much Californians liked to ride horses. Another tells of his own famous wedding.

Almost all the streets of Santa Barbara have Spanish names. Many have names of famous early-day families. Some of the old adobe homes are much as they once were. There is the De la Guerra house in El Paseo de la Guerra (sometimes called Street of Spain). There is El Cuartel, which is part of the old presidio. And there are other adobes on old ranchos nearby.

Californians still like to ride. Each spring about five hundred of them ride from rancho to rancho. They visit ranchos from Santa Barbara to Mission Santa Inés. That is why they are called *rancheros visitadores* (ranch visitors). This is another way in which Santa Barbara shows that it remembers its rancho days more than any other place in California.

Don Jose kept his books and a chest of money in the tower

83

MONTEREY

WHERE HISTORY WAS MADE AND LIFE WAS GAY

During both the Spanish and Mexican periods, Monterey was the military and social capital of California. The first grant of land was made by Spain as early as 1775. It was given to a soldier who married an Indian girl at Mission San Carlos. After that, pueblo lots in Monterey were given to settlers who promised to build homes. Twenty years later there were about six large ranchos nearby.

Something exciting was always happening in Monterey during those days! Sometimes there was a celebration because a ship came into the harbor. Boston ships came to pay duty on their goods. Sometimes famous visitors came, and that was reason enough for a celebration. The gayest time of all was when a new governor came. The cannon at the presidio was the first to boom a welcome. Soldiers in red and blue marched to the plaza with flags flying. Then everyone went to the home of the governor. Señoritas of famous families bowed before the governor. In return he gave them gifts or boxes of candy. Then came a feast spread on tables in the plaza. People wanted to show the new governor how fine the food was in California! Beef was sent from the ranchos near Monterey. Fruit came from the Santa Clara Valley. Ranchos in the south sent fruit and wine made from their vineyards. "This is wonderful food indeed!" he said. Then they showed him the kind of sports they had. A bear-and-bull fight followed. Governors seemed to like Monterey. One said, "This is a great country—neither hot nor cold. To live long, with little care, one must come to Monterey!" Governors soon found they did not have to work hard. People had few laws. What laws they had, they obeyed.

Most people liked to live in Monterey. But there were those who liked to live on their ranchos nearby. During the rainy season there was not much to do on the ranchos. "It is time to go to Monterey again," a ranchero would tell his wife. "It will give us

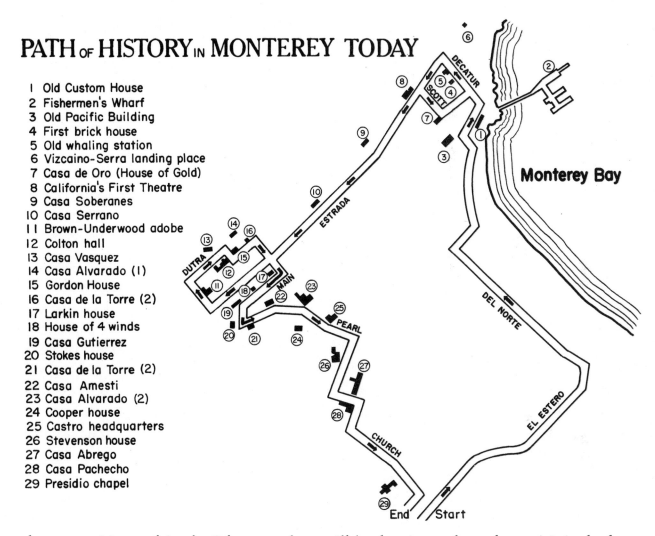

PATH of HISTORY in MONTEREY TODAY

1 Old Custom House
2 Fishermen's Wharf
3 Old Pacific Building
4 First brick house
5 Old whaling station
6 Vizcaino-Serra landing place
7 Casa de Oro (House of Gold)
8 California's First Theatre
9 Casa Soberanes
10 Casa Serrano
11 Brown-Underwood adobe
12 Colton hall
13 Casa Vasquez
14 Casa Alvarado (1)
15 Gordon House
16 Casa de la Torre (2)
17 Larkin house
18 House of 4 winds
19 Casa Gutierrez
20 Stokes house
21 Casa de la Torre (2)
22 Casa Amesti
23 Casa Alvarado (2)
24 Cooper house
25 Castro headquarters
26 Stevenson house
27 Casa Abrego
28 Casa Pachecho
29 Presidio chapel

Monterey Bay

DECATUR
SCOTT
ESTRADA
DUTRA
MAIN
PEARL
DEL NORTE
EL ESTERO
CHURCH
End Start

a chance to visit our friends. Of course there will be dancing—there always is! And who knows—maybe a Boston trading ship will be in!" After the visit, they were ready to go back to the rancho. By that time the grass was tall and the cattle were fat. There was work to be done on the ranchos once more. But the rancheros always went back to Monterey when they could.

In 1832 a Yankee trader, Thomas Larkin, landed in California. The newcomer was welcomed by the people. Soon he had their good will. He quickly learned the Spanish language. But there was one thing about them he did not understand. They said, "There is always tomorrow—*mañana! Mañana*—and *poco tiempo*—tomorrow and after a while! "That is all right for those Spanish people," he said. "Not for me! I must move fast!" And that is why he grew rich.

The people of Monterey soon found that Boston ships brought fine goods. Larkin was quick to see what they needed. If they didn't know what they wanted, he saw to it that they found out! Hardware, calico, *mantillas,* or shawls! He knew their love of color and finery. If they wanted something special, he ordered it. He could get it from Mexico or Boston in ten months. That was not long to wait! In return he took otter skins, hides, and tallow—no money. He sold the skins and tallow to the ships at high prices. The new trader soon had the biggest business on the coast.

Thomas Larkin married an American widow. She did not understand the Spanish language. She did not know the Spanish ways. But the people of Monterey made her welcome. Even the governor made a speech at the wedding feast. Soon after that, Larkin and his wife left Monterey for a while. When they came back, Larkin built a large two-story house. It was different from any the people had seen. It had a porch across the second story. All houses built like this from rancho days to the present time are called "Monterey houses."

Monterey became famous for its *cascarón* balls. They were usually given just before Easter. Women put on their finest dresses. They wore ruffled skirts and graceful shawls. From their high combs hung lacy white or black *mantillas.* The men wore their best velvet suits. For days people were busy making *cascarones.* Holes were made in the ends of eggs. The insides of the eggs were blown out. Then the eggshells were filled with bright pieces of paper or with perfume. The holes were sealed with wax or paper. Then the *cascarones* were put in a basket, ready for the ball. Everyone was excited when the *cascarones* were brought in. Young men broke them over the heads of the señoritas. Bits

Houses built like Larkin's home are still called "Monterey houses"

Forty-eight men came to Colton Hall to make the first California Constitution

The Old Custom House is the oldest government building in California

of paper floated over their long, black hair. Crack! another *cascarón* was broken! This time, perfume trickled down the nose of a young man!

In 1842 the peace of Monterey seemed to end. The governor had gone south on a visit. An American ship anchored in the harbor. Someone saw a strange flag flying over the Custom House. It was an American flag. "What does this mean?" said the people of Monterey. The American officer told them, "Have no fear. We mean no harm. Your rights will not be taken away from you." But Larkin hurried out to see the captain of the American ship. Captain Jones told him what had happened. "I came to a port in Mexico," he said. "There I heard the United States was at war with Mexico. I thought that England might slip in and try to take California. So here I am instead—to take California for the United States!" "But," said Larkin to the captain, "here are letters I have just received. Nothing is said about any war. You must be wrong!" Captain Jones decided that Larkin was right. Down went the American flag he had put up. Before the ship sailed, Larkin had a grand ball for the men. "Come," said Captain Jones, "now we will have a feast and dance on our ship!" So there was merrymaking instead of war!

The next year Larkin received a letter from Washington. It said, "You are to be the first United States Consul." That meant that he was to take care of all American affairs in California. He was to do what he could to make the Californians friendly to the United States. He hoped that they might want California to become part of the United States. Some of them thought this would be wise. Others did not.

More and more Americans were coming to California. They did not understand the Spanish people. They did not trust or like them at first. The Californians had much the same feeling about the Americans who came. Then one day an American officer, John C. Frémont, came to Monterey. The people were excited when they saw the soldiers with him ."Did you ever see so many soldiers?" they said. "Just look at their coats and hats of fur! They look more like animals than men! What are they doing here?" Frémont said that they had come to see California and make maps. But Larkin knew that these men really meant to take California. He told Frémont and his men that they could stay a short time only. So they left for the north. The people of Monterey heard that they went to Sonoma. They heard that they raised the Bear Flag there. They had declared California a republic, free from Mexico. But the republic lasted only three weeks. On July 7, 1846, an American ship sailed into Monterey harbor. Almost before the people knew what had happened, the American flag was flying over the presidio on the hill.

It was in 1849 that the great rush for gold began. Not many left to go to the gold fields. The people in Monterey had what they wanted—and all they wanted. Larkin knew the miners would need supplies, food, and clothes. "There are other ways to get gold," he told the people. So they stayed in Monterey and sold the things the miners needed.

By the end of that year thousands of new settlers came to California. These Americans knew little about Spanish California laws. Before California could become a state, it had to have a set of rules. The people who came wanted American laws for California. Something had to be done. The new American governor decided to have a meeting. He asked each town to choose men to come to Monterey. Forty-eight men met in Colton Hall. Don José Antonio Carrillo and Pablo de la Guerra came from the south. Mariano Vallejo came from Sonoma. John Sutter came from his fort. John C. Frémont was there and, of course, Thomas Larkin. These men worked hard to make good laws for the state. The set of rules they made was called a constitution. When they were all through, they sent a copy of it to Washington. Men were sent to ask that California be made a state in the United States. Month after month passed. At last the President signed a paper. "California is now the thirty-first state of the United States," it said.

At first life in Monterey went on much as it always had. Spanish was still the language most people knew. But even so—a great new state was in the making. Monterey's days as a capital were almost over. San José became the new capital. Monterey became once more a sleepy village.

Monterey still lives with its memories of Spanish days. At the center of Old Monterey is Colton Hall and the Friendly Plaza. The Old Custom House is still there by the bay.

It is the oldest government building in California. Here three nations have flown their flags—Spain, Mexico, and the United States. Nearly fifty old adobe or sandstone houses still remain. People are proud of the old adobes and care for them. There are lines in the streets that guide visitors to the places of interest. If one knew the stories of these places, he would know the story of early California history.

New Monterey is quite different from Old Town. On the coast are many fishing wharves. All through the night, lights flicker in the bay. In the morning, the fishermen come in with their catch. The blue-shirted men laugh and talk as they spread brown nets in the sun. Down the long curve of the coast are other cities. There are lovely beaches with white sand and rocky cliffs. Behind are hills covered with pines and twisted cypress trees. It is easy to see why the early Californians liked Monterey. From everywhere people come to see the famous buildings. They stay to enjoy the beautiful places and the mild climate. To all who come, Monterey gives a real welcome as in the old days.

On top was a cock that turned with the wind

SAN FRANCISCO
WHERE GOLD MADE A CITY AND CHANGED THE RANCHOS

Early Spanish explorers had told of a great harbor on the coast of California. They had marked it on their maps. "This is not one harbor, but many," they said. "Spain must keep it! To keep it, a fort must be built—and soon!" But Spain knew there must be not only a fort. Not just soldiers living at forts or presidios. Not only friars and Indians living at missions. Farmers must come with their wives and children. The Viceroy in Mexico said, "A colony must be started by this bay at once!" The rulers of Spain and Mexico decided that Juan de Anza, a wise and brave soldier, should start the colony.

So it was that two months later, a crowd gathered in a plaza in Mexico. On a tree was a strange letter. No one read it, for few knew how to read. Some said the name of Juan de Anza was at the end. Soon Captain Anza stood by the tree and faced the people. In a strong voice he said, "I want you to go with me! Nothing here will ever be any better. You will always be poor. Your land will not grow what you need. But this new land—this New California—ah! There land waits for hands to plant crops. Look at your crops drying in the fields. There you would have a harvest of golden grain. This land will be a place of plenty for you—and your children!"

No one seemed to be interested at first. He offered them food and clothing if they would go. One man in the crowd said, "Captain, we would like to go, but we might starve. It is too long a journey." Captain Anza told them how he had led twenty men over the desert the year before. "I promise that all who go will reach California. When you get there, I will see that you have cattle—horses—land! Now who goes?" At last more than two hundred agreed to go with him. The day came for them to leave for the new land. Soldiers led the way through the streets of Tubac. The settlers for New California followed on their horses. Half of the company were children. Pack mules plodded along behind. At the end came the black cattle, stirring up clouds of dust.

It was a terrible journey. The great company moved slowly. They crossed a thousand miles of desert lands. It was winter, and there were days and nights of cold as they crossed the mountains. Several times there was no water. All of the party were hungry most of the time. Then one day there seemed to be a change. Instead of rocks and dry plants, everything looked green. They knew they were not far from San Gabriel in southern California. They were safe in this new land at last! Anza wanted to tell them how brave they were. But he waited, for the long journey was not over. On New Year's Day they saw the walls of Mission San Gabriel. The padres came out to meet them. The bells clanged a welcome. People shouted with happiness. Soon sheep were roasted over burning coals for the hungry travelers.

After a month they were ready to start on the last part of the journey. One morning they saw a sight they had dreamed about—the sea! Then they came to Monterey one day in a dripping rain. As they came near the bay, they could hear the chapel bells ringing. Father Serra hurried over from Carmel to welcome them. While the people rested, Anza went on to San Francisco Bay. He and his men went with the padres to find places for a presidio and a mission. Back of the hills they came to a lake and a little stream. They decided to have a mission there. A place was found for the presidio too. It was on a high hill near the entrance to the harbor. Anza hurried back to Monterey to tell the others about their new home.

Anza had to go back to Mexico. Sadly, the people watched their captain ride down the trail that led back to Tubac. Young Lieutenant Moraga led them on to the place they were to live by the bay. In was in March, 1776, that they looked over the largest bay they had ever seen. The soldiers and some of the settlers stayed here to build the presidio and small houses. The rest of the settlers went on over the hill to a place chosen for Mission San Francisco.

At first, ships that came into the bay anchored near the presidio. But a cove was found that was deep and quiet. Here was a sandy beach where small boats from a ship

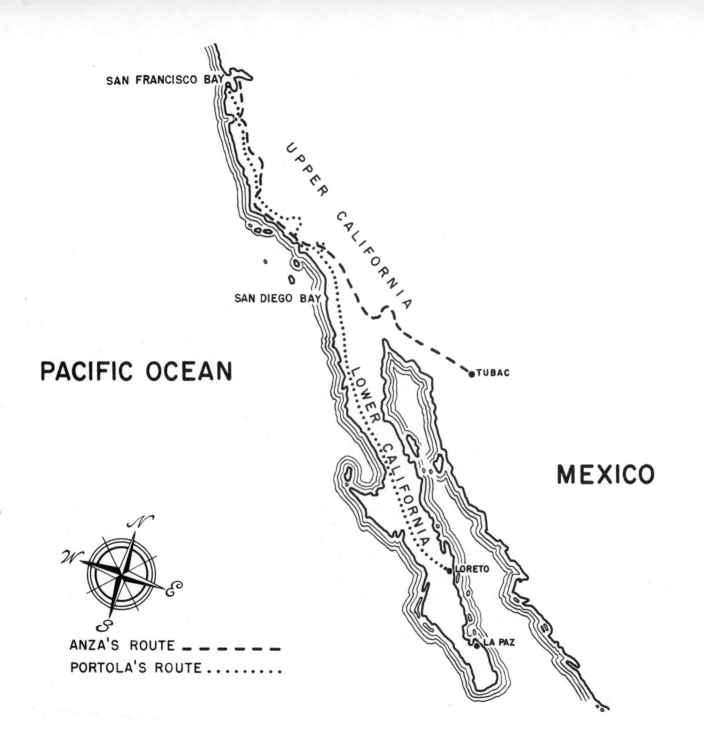

SAN FRANCISCO BAY

UPPER CALIFORNIA

SAN DIEGO BAY

PACIFIC OCEAN

LOWER CALIFORNIA

TUBAC

MEXICO

LORETO

LA PAZ

N
W E
S

ANZA'S ROUTE ‒ ‒ ‒ ‒
PORTOLA'S ROUTE . . . .

could land easily. Away from the strong winds, the cove was a safer place for ships to anchor. It was halfway between the presidio and the mission. Everyone who came saw the sweet-smelling vine growing there. So the place was called Yerba Buena (Good Herb). Red deer made their way to the springs near the cove. Quail ran quickly in and out of the scrub-oak bushes. Sometimes there were footprints of bears in the mud.

Not many ships came into the harbor. Spanish ships came to trade. A few French and English ships stopped to explore. Whaling ships came into the harbor. These ships usually came from New England. They had made long journeys to the north to find whales. They needed a place to land where ships could be repaired. Sailors needed fresh food and a chance to rest. They found another cove in the bay where they liked to stay. The sailors called it Whaler's Bay (now Sausalito). They were quick to see that money could be made easily. They took otter skins and gave the people goods in exchange. In the next few years, many ships came in and out of the coves, flying the American flag.

Most of those who came with Captain Anza later became rancheros. One of them was Don Luis Peralta. He was given a very large rancho on the east side of the bay. At first he thought he wanted many acres of land. But after he had lands and a big house, he changed his mind. One day he said to his four sons, "I do not like to be a rich man. I like my little rancho near Mission San Jose. You boys can have this big Rancho San Antonio." So one day they rode out together. To each son he gave one fourth of his land from the bay to the hills. As years went by, Rancho San Antonio became three large cities—Oakland, Berkeley, and Alameda.

Two rancheros built their homes about the same time. These men were very different, but they became good friends. José Amador's father had come with Portolá, the explorer. His friend, Don Roberto Livermore, had been an English sailor. Don José did not want to raise cattle just to sell hides and tallow. He wanted to make saddles, harness, and shoes from the hides. He used tallow to make hundreds of pounds of soap and candles. And he became a rich man. Don José kept adding to his Rancho San Ramón. Finally his rancho became one of the largest in California. Roberto Livermore used his

The Russians built a fort, a church and houses north of San Francisco Bay

rancho in a different way too. In the fertile valley he planted the first wheat. He laid out a vineyard at his Rancho *Las Positas* (Little Wells). But his pride was in his orchards. People used to say, "We would go miles to eat Don Roberto's apples and pears!" The names of these rancheros are still remembered. There is the Amador Valley, Amador County, and the town of Livermore—all reminders of the friends who lived side by side.

Another ranchero came as an English sailor on a whaling ship. As soon as Captain Richardson came ashore, he knew he wanted to stay. He promised to become a useful citizen. First he taught the Spaniards how to make boats. Help was needed in another way. There were rocky shores at the entrance to the bay. Richardson taught Indians how to guide ships between the rocks, safely into port. Not long after that he was made captain of the port. One day he sat watching the slow oxcarts going down the muddy roads. It took them a week to go to San Jose and back. He thought there should be a quicker way to carry supplies than that. So he did something about it. He built small boats that took supplies and people across the bay.

Don William Richardson was granted Rancho Saucelito (present Sausalito). But he did not like to live on his rancho. It was his plan to found a port town on the bay. He took his family to live at the Yerba Buena cove. He built the first shelter there made of redwood posts covered with a ship's sail. The only neighbors they had were bears, coyotes, and wolves. The nearest people were at the mission or the presidio. Then he built a board house (in about the center of present-day Chinatown in San Francisco). The house had a store in it and became a small trading post.

As the years passed, Yerba Buena became a village of about two hundred people. First the Spanish flag and then the Mexican flag flew over the presidio on the hill. After the war with Mexico, the American flag was raised. The next year, in 1847, the name of the town was changed from Yerba Buena to San Francisco.

In the year 1848 there was exciting news in California. Gold was found at Sutter's Mill. It was spring when the news came to the coast towns. Soon, one by one, men were missing. Where were they going? many began to wonder. Then one morning a man came running into the plaza (Portsmouth Square) in San Francisco. In his hand he had a whole bottle of gold dust. "Gold!" he called in a loud voice. "See, pure gold, I tell you! Gold from the American River!" That settled it! Excitement grew and grew. The news set men wild! Each one wanted his share of gold. In a few days hardly a man was left around the bay. Stores closed. Fields were left half planted. Houses were left half built. Sailors left their ships. Soldiers left the presidio. Signs on doors said, "Gone to the gold fields." Some went on horses; some on foot. But all were in a hurry to get to a place called Coloma by the American River. By summer, only women, children, and old men were left.

San Francisco became the talk of the world! Ships going to other countries took the news. A California newspaper told the story. Word went all over the United States. Wherever the word "gold" was heard, people were excited. "Gold picked up in the streams! Gold for everyone! Was there ever anything like that? Let's head for California!" And hundreds came, first by ships. There were not enough ships for those who wished to go. The once sleepy little town at the cove changed swiftly. Once there were many twisted oaks and patches of wild-mint vine there. Now the brown hills were lined with hundreds of tents. There were just a few adobe buildings and some wooden ones. Most of the houses were made of rough boards. Even old ships were used for homes or stores. One old ship was even used as a prison.

The cove was filled with ships. But no sailors stayed on board. As soon as ships came, the men were off to the mountains. Some of them took little boats up the Sacramento River. Everyone thought that gold could be found in all the streams. So they started out on rivers. A good place to stop for supplies was Sutter's Fort. Another place to get tools and food on the way was Tuleberg. So Sutter's Fort and Tuleberg became trading centers. Later they became the cities of Sacramento and Stockton.

Some wise ones did not go to the gold fields. They saw a chance to make money an easier way. One of them was Don Luis Peralta. He called his sons to him one day. "My sons," he said, "let the Americans have their gold. Plant your lands. Sell your crops.

98

These are richer than gold fields! All must eat while they live!" And he was right. Food prices went higher and higher. Gold dust was used for money. Flour was forty dollars a barrel. Eggs were a dollar each. Then how much was meat? Plenty! No reason to sell hides and tallow now! Meat was worth much more. "Guess the days of trading ships are about over!" the old rancheros said. "Our storekeepers are making even more than the miners! And a lot easier too!"

There was one man who did not become rich because of gold. That was Captain John Sutter. Gold-seekers took almost everything he had. They cut down his trees and killed his cattle. People settled on his land and would not get off. He left for the East and died a poor man. The gold that was easy to find was soon gone. The men had to go farther. They had to dig deeper into the mountains and streams. Still gold-seekers came by the thousands. When they did not find gold, they looked for something else. They did not want to return. All were looking toward future days. All wanted to be rich. So they decided to get land. The easiest way was to stay on the land and not get off. These people were called "squatters." There were land-grabbers everywhere. Many of the finest ranchos around the bay were lost this way.

By the end of 1849 there were thousands of new settlers in California. San Francisco was no longer a city of tents and little wooden buildings. There were many large business buildings and houses. The harbor was full of ships. Then in 1850, San Francisco heard news almost as exciting as that of gold! An American ship, the *Oregon*, sailed into the bay. "Boom!" thundered the signal gun on board. The American flag flew high on the mast. A long banner on the ship said, "California, a state!" Now the ship's bells rang. Cannons in Portsmouth Square boomed! So did the cannons at the presidio. So did every cannon on every ship in the bay. People shouted with joy! People crowded into the streets. Nobody did any work that day. There were bands, dancing, and music everywhere! Fireworks and bonfires lit up the night. Riders carried the news to the new capital at San Jose. Soon the Stars and Stripes flew on all the flagpoles of the city and the state. San Francisco was no longer a Spanish town. It was no longer just a place for whaling ships to anchor. It was an American city in a new American state. And on September 9, the first Admission Day, there was a celebration over all the seven hills. The days of the ranchos were about over.

The presidio, the mission, and the cove of Yerba Buena—all became one great city. Ships from all over the world sail in and out through the Golden Gate. John C. Frémont gave this name to the entrance of the bay. Where trading ships and whalers used to come are huge wharves. Where little boats crossed the bay are great bridges, the largest in the world!

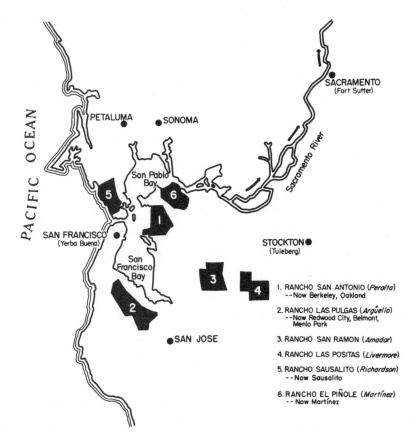

1. RANCHO SAN ANTONIO (*Peralta*)
--Now Berkeley, Oakland

2. RANCHO LAS PULGAS (*Arguello*)
--Now Redwood City, Belmont, Menlo Park

3. RANCHO SAN RAMON (*Amador*)

4. RANCHO LAS POSITAS (*Livermore*)

5. RANCHO SAUSALITO (*Richardson*)
--Now Sausalito

6. RANCHO EL PIÑOLE (*Martínez*)
--Now Martínez

MARIANO VALLEJO
AND HOW HE BECAME OWNER OF A GREAT VALLEY IN THE NORTH

"Forward march! Left-right, left-right! Halt!" The soldiers' heels clicked to a quick stop. The boy, Mariano Vallejo, watched the soldiers marching in the plaza at Monterey. "I want to be a soldier like that," he said to himself. If he were a soldier, he could wear a blue and red uniform. He might even become an officer as his father had. How proud he would be then!

"First of all, I want you to have other training," Sergeant Vallejo told his sons. "There is a new school here in Monterey. You must go there to learn to read and write. At home you can learn trades—pottery and brick making, tanning of hides, making of soap and candles. There will be time for horseback riding and dancing—if you do all the other things well."

When Mariano was sixteen years old, he became a soldier at the presidio. He worked so hard for four years that he became an officer. Once the governor sent him north where the Indians were making trouble. Once he sent him on special business to San Diego. It pleased Mariano to go to San Diego. Everyone knew that it was a gay and friendly place. He was not a stranger there very long. He rode with the men, danced with the señoritas, and went to *meriendas* almost every day. Of all the charming young ladies, Señorita Carrillo pleased him the most. Before he left San Diego, Don Joaquín Carrillo had said, "Mariano, you may marry my daughter, Francisca, someday. Remember, though, you are a soldier. You must send word to the Viceroy of Mexico. If he says you may marry—then I say you may too!" "I will write at once," said Don Mariano happily. He knew it would take many months.

While Francisca waited, she was very busy. She and her mother and sisters embroidered and sewed every day. Don Mariano sent beautiful presents to her too. He did as all bridegrooms did in those days. He sent her six of everything. There was six *mantillas,* six shawls, and six pairs of shoes. The beads and earrings he sent matched the silk dresses given by her father.

A year and a half passed. A letter from Mariano came telling Francisca to get ready for the wedding. He wanted it to be the finest ever seen in California. Even the governor was invited. On the day of the wedding a gay company rode up a winding trail to the church. Don Juan Bandini had the honor of taking the bride to the wedding. They rode together on his white horse. As she rode sideways, one foot rested in a loop of satin. Almost all brides went to their weddings this way. Francisca's dress of yellow satin matched the sunshine of the day. Flowers made a circle of color on her black hair. Don Mariano, the family, and friends rode along behind. After the wedding, Francisca rode back with Don Mariano on his horse. As they went there were whispers, "Lucky Francisca. Isn't Don Mariano handsome—and a fine soldier too!"

Everyone joined in the feast given for them at the large Bandini home. The governor made a speech of good wishes. Soon after that, the governor told Mariano that he wanted him to go north. Indians were causing trouble. There was another reason too. A new governor was coming to Monterey. Mariano did not want to leave Francisca, of course. Being a soldier, he knew it was his duty. After a few days he left for the north.

Eight months passed by. Don Mariano was too busy to come back for Francisca. He had become *comandante* of the presidio at San Francisco. So he sent his brother to San Diego to bring Francisca to him. All San Diego came to say good-by to her as she left. Church bells rang. Children threw flowers in her path as she rode away. Francisca had never been on such a long journey before. Each night they were made welcome at the nearest rancho. Every day Francisca became a little more excited. One morning the sun shone through a bank of fog. She could see the blue-gray waters of San Francisco Bay! It was not long after that she reached her new home. She was glad to be with Don Mariano, but San Diego seemed very far away.

Soon after she came to San Francisco, Don Mariano was sent farther north. The

Vallejo built the largest house in all of California

Russians had been living at Fort Ross, not very far away. A fort, a church, and houses had been built near a little cove in the sea. The Russians became rich from the otter furs they found there. The land gave them grain and other crops. It was easy to see that they planned to stay. Perhaps they might come farther south. "Stop the Russians in the north!" the governor said to Mariano. "Explore the land near there. Make friends with the Indians. Perhaps you can even start a new pueblo. Later, we will give land to all the people who wish to live there."

General Vallejo rode proudly at the head of the company of soldiers. On the way he saw rich pasture lands. There were deep-flowing streams of water. "This would be a wonderful place for ranchos!" he thought. The farther north he went, the more

103

beautiful the country seemed. He came out of the Napa Valley and climbed a low mountain range. Below lay the Valley of the Moon—Sonoma, the Indians called it. Suddenly the company halted at the doors of the old mission.

Vallejo knew he had to make friends with the Indians. No one would ever come to live in the north if the Indians were unfriendly. Not far from the mission were Chief Solano and three thousand Indians. General Vallejo became a friend of the chief. He agreed that the Indians there would cause no trouble.

The next thing General Vallejo did was to lay out plans for a new pueblo. In the center was a plaza where the flag of Mexico would fly. Here the soldiers would march every day. It would remind him of the days when he used to watch the soldiers in Monterey. A large home was built for the soldiers on one side of the plaza. Don Mariano built a two-story home for Francisca. At one end was a tower so he could see everything that went on in the plaza. Then he sent for Francisca to come north. "There is no place so beautiful as the Valley of the Moon," he said.

Vallejo now sent out word, "Come to Sonoma! There is free land for the asking! Indians will help clear the land. Indians will build your home. Tools will be given for planting. The storerooms of the mission are full of grain and seeds. Come get your land!" And people did come asking for land. Vallejo welcomed all strangers who came. People lived in the old mission building while their homes were being built. Soon fields were being plowed for the first planting. Everyone thought how kind and generous Vallejo was! "I cannot use all the land anyway," he told himself. There was a more important reason. A pueblo would help keep other countries out of northern California.

Some people said that Vallejo was too friendly to American strangers. He had reasons for being friendly to them. His sisters had married Americans. One American made shingles for the roof of his house. It was the first shingle roof in California. One taught his children how to play the piano. Another even went to England to get sheep for him. To all Americans who helped him he gave rancho lands.

One day Francisca said, "Mariano, our many children make this house seem small!

Several women ground corn on stone metates most of the day

Why not build a larger home in the country? You have given away hundreds of acres of land. Now give some to yourself!" Mariano chose a place not far away in the Petaluma Valley. "Let others raise their cattle and have their ranchos," he said. "I want an *hacienda*, a rancho where only crops are grown. I want to grow more crops than anyone in California! Not only that—I am going to have the biggest house in all of California!" And to be sure, he should have the largest house. He was now the richest man in California!

Francisca Vallejo was never lonely on her *hacienda*. There was always so much to do! Most of her time was spent showing the many Indians how to work. There were fifty-six servants working all the time in the house. There was a servant for each of her fourteen children. Each Indian was taught to do one thing and do it well. Five or six Indians washed clothes every day. Several did nothing but grind corn on the stone *metates*. The pounding was the first sound to be heard in the morning. It was usually heard all day. Other servants did nothing but make *tortillas*. They hummed together, keeping time with the pat-pat of their baking all day long. There was the pleasant smell of browning beef from the kitchen. "We give the Indians all the food they need, too," said Doña Francisca. "We give them no pay. If they are sick, we care for them. We treat them as our friends."

Days came when General Vallejo thought about the changes that were coming to California. The past days were happy days—but what was ahead. It was not long before he knew. One morning some Americans came to Sonoma carrying guns. They took their places around Vallejo's home. They told him that he was their prisoner. They said that General John Frémont had told them to do this. Vallejo could not understand the reason, but he was polite to them. The men were not sure what to do with their prisoner. Then it was agreed to take Vallejo, his brother, and a friend to Sutter's Fort. Before they left, they raised the Bear Flag of the California Republic over the plaza. As they rode away, Chief Solano watched from the distance. He could not understand what was happening. What had become of the Mexican flag? Why did not General

Hundreds of Indians plowed in the fields

Reminders of the Vallejo family are kept in the Swiss Chalet

Vallejo fight? He now felt lonely. His own people were gone. Now his great friend was gone too. He could help in only one way. He could take care of Francisca and the children while his friend was away.

The seventh of July in 1846 was a day to remember in more ways than one! That was the day the American flag was raised at Monterey. That same day was Vallejo's thirty-eighth birthday. Word came that he was to leave Sutter's Fort. Joyfully, he and the others turned toward home. The first thing he saw in the Sonoma plaza was the American flag flying! Vallejo made a pile of the soldiers' Mexican uniforms. He watched them burn to black ashes. "Now," he said proudly, "I have become a Yankee! From now on all Americans in California are my guests. Let them come!"

More and more strangers came to California. Some were famous; many were rich. Vallejo began to feel that his Petaluma home was not good enough. "After all, Francisca, it is made of mud. We need a better home now. We should have only the best for our guests. Nothing is too good for you. Our next house should look like an American house!" So he bought some land just north of the town of Sonoma. Clear water, hot and cold, ran from the hills nearby. Lachryma Montis (Mountain Tears), he called the new home. He spent money freely to build it. This time the adobe walls were covered with wood. Iron used in the house came from China. In every room were fireplaces made of stone. Thousands of dollars were spent for rugs and furniture. Hot and cold water from the springs was piped into the house. Whoever heard of such things in those days? Even the Americans could not believe it! A storeroom was needed and a place for the helpers. This time Vallejo sent to Switzerland for wood. Each piece of lumber came with a number on it. In this way it was put together just right. The Swiss chalet delighted both Francisca and her husband.

Then came people who settled on Vallejo's land and would not get off. "You would think the land belonged to them!" he said angrily. He had to stand by and see men cut down trees on his land. They plowed land that belonged to him. What could he do? Nothing but wait! A paper finally came from Washington. It said that the land belonged to him. He told the "squatters" the next morning. Still they would not get off his land. Finally he decided to give up. "What if they do take some of our lands, Francisca?" he said. "We still have plenty left. I had my day. It was a proud one too."

The Vallejo home in Sonoma may still be seen. The once proud Casa Grande where thousands of Indians worked, stands alone in the Petaluma Valley. A sign in front says:

OLD ADOBE, HISTORICAL LANDMARK,
STATE OF CALIFORNIA

The State of California also owns the beautifully kept home near Sonoma. Around the white house are the same fig and olive trees planted so long ago.

Mariano Vallejo used to say, "My family has served under three flags. We have lived on Spanish, Mexican, and United States soil. My wife and I were born under the flag of Spain. Fourteen of my children were born under the Mexican flag and two under the Stars and Stripes. We are all good Americans! But first of all we are true Californians!"

A GUIDE TO ADOBES AND LANDMARKS OF RANCHO DAYS

Rancho, Adobe, Landmark	Who Owned	When built	Where it is	Present use	Interesting to know
ALAMEDA COUNTY *Rancho San Antonio	Ygnacio Peralta	1860	San Leandro Cor. Cherrywood and E. 13th St.	Alta Mira Club House	First brick house in the county
CONTRA COSTA COUNTY R. Los Medanos (The Sand Dunes)	Dr. John Marsh	1856	4 mi. S.W. of Brentwood	Home	Dr. Marsh was first doctor in the San Joaquin Valley. Murdered by Indians who thought him unkind
*R. del Diablo (Ranch of the Devil)	Salvio Pacheco	1844	Concord Cor. Concord and Salvio Ave.	Restaurant	Good example of a Spanish home
Gutiérrez Adobe	Candida and Jovita Castro	1850	Richmond S. bank of Arroyo Grande, just N.W. of San Pablo	Home	Schooners used to come up creek to back door. Brought supplies and took away products of the rancho
R. San Pablo	Son of Francisco Castro	1838	San Pablo San Pablo and Church Sts.	Storeroom	Gov. Alvarado retired to this home and lived there for 35 years
KERN COUNTY *Fort El Tejon (The Badger)	U. S. Government	1854	Hwy. 99, 7 mi. N. of Gorman	Museum	Fort to protect Americans from Indians. Stopping place on old stage road
KINGS COUNTY R. Los Robles (Ranch of the Oaks)	Daniel Rhodes	1856	2 mi. N. of LeMoore, nr. Hanford	Home	First orchard in valley planted here. Carefully kept adobe home. Visitors by invitation
LOS ANGELES COUNTY *Casa de Adobe	Part of Southwest Museum		Los Angeles 4605 N. Figueroa	Open to public Wed. & Sun. 2–5 No charge	Replica of a Spanish ranch house. Furnished as in rancho days. Exhibits of branding irons, clothing, etc., of that period
*Avila Adobe	Francisco Avila	1818	Los Angeles Olvera St., just N. of plaza, nr. Main and Sunset	Open to public Small charge	Oldest and most historic building in L. A.

*Open to the public

A GUIDE TO ADOBES AND LANDMARKS OF RANCHO DAYS

Rancho, Adobe, Landmark	Who Owned	When built	Where it is	Present use	Interesting to know
*Campo de Cahuenga		1848–52	Los Angeles 3919 Lankershim Blvd.	Open to public Mon.–Fri. 9–5	Site where Gen. Andrés Pico and Gen. John C. Frémont signed peace treaty between U. S. and Mexico
*R. La Brea	1st—Antonio Rocha Later—Hancock family	1828–30	Los Angeles 5000 block, Wilshire Blvd.	Given as park to L. A. City by Geo. Allan Hancock	Prehistoric animals found in the tar pits. People of pueblo used to get tar here for their roofs
*Pico House	Pio Pico	1869	Los Angeles N. Main St., S. of plaza	Offices	Site of old Carrillo home. First 3-story building in L. A. Best hotel of that time
*Plaza Church (Church of the Angeles)		1818–22	Los Angeles Main and Sunset, W. side of plaza	Church	Oldest church in L. A., still in daily use
R. Rincon de los Bueyes (Corner of the Oxen)	1st—Bernardo Higuero Later—Antonio José Rocha, son of owner of R. La Brea	1860?	Los Angeles David & Shenandoah Sts.	Home	School children in district visit on invitation
*R. Santa Anita	Hugo and Victoria Reid	1839	Arcadia Foothill Blvd. to Santa Fe depot, 1 mi. E. of Rosemead. Turn S. to L.A. Co. & State Arboretum	Open to public State property	First owner was Claudio Lopez, *mayordomo* of Mission San Gabriel. He named rancho for his friend, Anita Cota
R. San Antonio	Antonio Lugo	1850	Bell Cor. Gage & Downey 2½ mi. E. of Bell	Home & auto court	Country home of the Lugo family. Has always been occupied by member of the family since rancho days
*R. El Encino (Ranch of the Live Oak)	1st—Francisco Reyes, alcalde in L. A. 2nd—3 Indians 3rd—Vicente de la Osa Later—Amestoy family	1840	Encino Balboa St., just off Ventura Blvd.	Open to public State property	Portolá's party camped at this place. First house built in S.W. part of San Fernando Valley. Once used by padres of Mission San Fernando. First stage stop out of L. A.
*R. San Rafael	María Sepúlveda Sanchez, daughter of Rafael Verdugo	1872?	Glendale 1330 Dorothy Dr.	Open to public every aft. but Mon. Owned by City of Glendale	Shows simple, early California ranch house. Visitors can see home as it was then

111

A GUIDE TO ADOBES AND LANDMARKS OF RANCHO DAYS

Rancho, Adobe, Landmark	Who Owned	When built	Where it is	Present use	Interesting to know
R. San Rafael	Catalina Verdugo	1860	Glendale 2211 Bonita, cor. of Camulos	Home	Where blind Catalina Verdugo lived with her nephew. Tree in yard under which Gen. Pico and Gen. Frémont met
*R. Aguaje de Centinela (Water of the Sentinel)	1st—Ygnacio Machado 2nd—Bruno and Antonio Avila	about 1840	Inglewood 7634 Midfield, 300 yds. W. of Freeman Blvd.	Open to public	Machado traded this rancho and 2 barrels of brandy for his house in the pueblo of L. A.
R. Los Cerritos (Little Hills)	Part of Manuel Nieto's first Spanish grant (1784)	1844	Long Beach 6400 N. American, just N. of Virginia Country Club	Home	Country home of Juan Temple and wife, Rafaela Cota, from whose family he bought the land. One of the largest of old rancho houses. Temple St. in L. A. named for Juan Temple, rancho-day merchant
R. Los Alamitos (Little Cottonwood Trees)	1st—Manuel Nieto Later—Don Abel Stearns	1842	Long Beach State Hwy. 22, just E. of U. S. Naval Hosp.	Home	Country home of Don Abel Stearns and wife, Arcadia Bandini. Each year there was horse racing between this rancho and El Cerrito, the race being from Signal Hill straight to the beach
R. La Merced (The Gift)	Doña María Soto	1829	Montebello Intersection Merced and Lincoln Blvd.	Home	14-room adobe home, very well preserved
*R. Paso de Bartolo Viejo (Ranchito)	Pio Pico	1830's	Pico Whittier and Pioneer Blvds.	Open to public 10–5 except Mon. & Tues. State property	Home of the last Mexican governor of Calif. and the home he loved the most
R. San José	Ygnacio Palomares	1837	Pomona 1569 N. Park Ave.	Home	Second house built by Ygnacio Palomares
*R. San José	Ygnacio Palomares	about 1850	North Pomona 491 E. Cucamonga, cor. Orange Grove	Open to public Thurs. & Sun. aft. State property	Stagecoaches passed here on way to L.A. Adobe furnished and restored by City of Pomona and Pomona Valley Historical Soc.

112

A GUIDE TO ADOBES AND LANDMARKS OF RANCHO DAYS

Rancho, Adobe, Landmark	Who Owned	When built	Where it is	Present use	Interesting to know
R. San José	Ygnacio Alvarado	1840	Pomona 1475 N. Park Ave.	Home	Given to Alvarado by Ygnacio Palomares. Unusual to have close neighbors. Had chapel for services in his home
R. La Puente (The Bridge)	William Workman	1841–43	On knoll overlooking Puente Valley, about 1 mi. W. of Puente	Home	Came with Workman-Rowland Party (1841) from New Mexico. Both given ranchos. Travelers stopped here for rest and supplies. Had long tunnel under house where money was probably kept
R. San José de Arriba (Upper San José)	Saturnino Carrion	about 1850	2 mi. S. of San Dimas, via S. Walnut on Mt. Meadows Rd.	Home	Rancho given to Carrion when he was 11 years old by his uncle, Ygnacio Palomares
R. Ex-Mission San Fernando	Andrés Pico	1873	San Fernando ¼ mi. S. W. of Mission San Fernando	Home	Andrés Pico and nephew, Romolo, lived here. Once land was called Pico Reserve. Adobe is fine example of large Spanish home
Lopez Adobe	Juan Lopez	1792–1806	San Gabriel 330 S. Santa Anita	Home	Beautifully preserved. Called "Casa Vieja de Lopez" (Old Lopez House)
Ortega-Vigare Adobe	Ortega-Vigare family	1854	San Gabriel 616 Ramona St.	Home	Probably once a mission building. Built of leftover materials from first mission
Evertsen Adobe	Evertsen (surveyor)	1851	San Gabriel 725 Carmelita, just off Mission Blvd.	Home	Handmade doors
Gen. Howard Adobe	Mission building	1776	328 E. Mission Dr.	Home	Named after Gen. Volney Erskine Howard, who lived in it 1852–80

A GUIDE TO ADOBES AND LANDMARKS OF RANCHO DAYS

Rancho, Adobe, Landmark	Who Owned	When built	Where it is	Present use	Interesting to know
El Molino Viejo (The Old Mill)	Old Mill used by Mission San Gabriel	1818	San Marino 1120 Old Mill Rd.	Home	First gristmill in So. Calif. It proved useless because wheat became wet. Once used as storehouse and jail. Story that padres kept treasures there, but none ever found
*R. San Isidro	Michael White, English sailor	1845	San Marino 1 block E. of City Hall, on opp. side of Huntington Dr., behind school	Open to public, used by the school	White had large vineyard on the land. He married daughter of Doña Eulalia of Mission San Gabriel.
*R. San Pedro	Gen. Phineas Banning	1858	Wilmington Banning Park	Open to public Landmark 147	He founded town of Wilmington. House shows American influence following rancho days. Huge wistaria vine planted in early days still there
R. San Pedro	Manuel Domínguez	1826	San Pedro Alameda Blvd., 7½ mi. S. of Florence Ave., nr. Domínguez Junction	School for priests	Battle of Domínguez rancho fought here when American army tried to retake Los Angeles
R. San Pascual (Holy Easter)	José Perez, husband of Doña Eulalia of Mission San Gabriel	1839	South Pasadena 1801 Foothill Blvd. Nr. cor. of Grevelia and Garfield	Home	Home of Manuel and Luisa Avila Garfiás. Used as headquarters by Mexican Gen. Flores before Americans took California. Called Flores Adobe
MONTEREY COUNTY Casa Soberanes (House of the Blue Gate)	1st—José Estrada Later—Mariano Soberanes, son-in-law of Mariano Vallejo	1842	Monterey 314 Pacific St.	Home	Walls almost 3 ft. thick. The Vallejos often visited in this home
*Casa Serrano	Florencio Serrano	1845	Monterey Estrada and Franklin	Restaurant	Serrano was *alcalde* and schoolteacher in Monterey during the Mexican period

A GUIDE TO ADOBES AND LANDMARKS OF RANCHO DAYS

Rancho, Adobe, Landmark	Who Owned	When built	Where it is	Present use	Interesting to know
*Colton Hall	Rev. Walter Colton	1847–49	Monterey Bet. Jefferson and Madison (Friendly Plaza)	Open to public Upper floor, museum	Where California became a state. Meeting place of Constitutional Convention, 1849
Vasquez Adobe	Sister of bandit, Tiburcio Vasquez	?	Monterey 546 Dutra St.	Home	Vasquez was the bandit who hated Americans, robbed and killed them up and down the state
Casa Alvarado	Juan Alvarado	1836	Monterey Dutra & Jefferson Sts.	Home	Home of Alvarado while he was governor of Calif.
*Old Custom House	Three nations flew flags over it—Spain, Mexico, U. S.	1814	Monterey Decatur St., overlooking Bay of Monterey	Open to public 10–5 Early Calif. museum	Second story added in 1841. Oldest public building in Calif. All ships to Calif. came here first to pay duty on goods
*Old Pacific Building	Built mostly by Thomas O. Larkin	1847	Monterey Cor. Scott & Calle Principal	Open to public 10–5	Once a sailors' hotel. In back is pit used for bear-and-bull fights
*First brick house	Duncan Dickinson	1848–49	Monterey 351 Decatur St.	Restaurant	He and family came to Calif. with the famous Donner party. Half of the party perished in the snow of Donner Pass
Old Whaling Station		about 1850	Monterey 391 Decatur St.	Private	Once a boardinghouse for sailors from whaling ships
*Casa de Oro (House of Gold)	Built by Mexican Gen. Castro for soldiers	1845	Monterey 200 Oliver St.	Open to public 10–5	Miners brought gold here for safekeeping. Now property of state
*California's first theatre	Jack Swan, English sailor	1845	Monterey S.E. cor. of Pacific & Scott Sts.	Open to public 10–5	Jack Swan let sailors have plays here. Theater has wooden curtain. Now state property
Gordon House	1st—Philip Roach, first American mayor of Monterey Later—Samuel Gordon	1849–50	Monterey Pierce St., next to Colton Hall	Private	First all-wood house in Calif. Brought from Australia to England to Monterey

A GUIDE TO ADOBES AND LANDMARKS OF RANCHO DAYS

Rancho, Adobe, Landmark	Who Owned	When built	Where it is	Present use	Interesting to know
Larkin House	Thomas O. Larkin	1835	Monterey Cor. of Jefferson & Calle Principal	Private	House that set the style of "Monterey houses" all over Calif. First wholesale and retail store in Monterey here. Later it was office of American Consul
*House of the Four Winds	Thomas O. Larkin	About 1834	Monterey Calle Principal & Madison (rear of Larkin House)	Monterey Women's Civic Club	Once used for Hall of Records. Name given because of weathervane on top
*Casa Gutiérrez	Joaquín Gutiérrez	1843	Monterey 590 Calle Principal	Monterey Foundation	Gutiérrez was governor of Calif. twice
Stokes House	1st—Señor Cano Later—Thomas Stokes	1835	Monterey 500 Hartnell	Private	Home became center of gay social life. *Sala* famous for its *cascarón* balls
*Casa de la Torre (House of the Tower)	José de la Torre	1841	Monterey 599 Polk St.	Bookshop	First federal court here
Casa Amesti	José Amesti, brother-in-law of Mariano Vallejo	1825	Monterey 516 Polk St.	Private	Home given to his daughter for a wedding present
*Cooper House	John Rogers Cooper (half brother of Thomas O. Larkin)	1829	Monterey 508 Munras St.	Lower floor, museum of early Calif.	Built for his bride, Encarnación Vallejo. Fine example of early Monterey home
*Casa Estrada	José Ramón Estrada	1828	Monterey 456 Tyler St.	Mission Inn (hotel)	Once known as St. Charles Hotel (1849)
*Casa Sanchez	Gil Sanchez	1843	Monterey 414 Alvarado St.	Store	He helped found Santa Clara College
*Stevenson House	1st—Rafael Gonzales Later—Home and store of Giradin family	1838	Monterey Houston St., bet. Pearl & Webster	Open to public 10–5 Owned by state	Also called the "French House" because of Giradin family. Gonzales was first Collector of Customs for Calif. Robert Louis Stevenson, writer, once roomed in this house
Casa Abrego	José Abrego	1835	Monterey N.W. cor. of Webster & Abrego	Private	Home famous for *cascarón* balls. Some of lumber in home came from wrecked ship

A GUIDE TO ADOBES AND LANDMARKS OF RANCHO DAYS

Rancho, Adobe, Landmark	Who Owned	When built	Where it is	Present use	Interesting to know
*Casa Munras	Esteban Munras, artist	1822	Monterey 656 Munras St.	Hotel	One of the first homes built outside old Spanish presidio walls
*Presidio Chapel of Monterey	Founded by Father Junípero Serra	1770–95	Monterey Church St.	Church	Only presidio church left in Calif., not a mission. Has been used ever since the founding
*Mission San Carlos	Founded by Father Junípero Serra	1770	Carmel Valley, nr. Monterey	Mission Church	Once the home of all missions in Calif. Father Serra and Father Crespi buried here
NAPA COUNTY R. Catacula	Joseph B. Chiles	1844	Chiles Valley, nr. Napa	Home	Near the river Chiles built a house and gristmill that are still there
*R. Tulucay	Cayento Juarez	1840's	1 mi. S.E. of Napa	Tavern	Juarez tried to free the Bear Flag prisoners; swam 9 mi. to escape
R. Yajome	Salvador Vallejo	1836	Nr. Napa on Longwood Ranch, nr. Napa River	Home	Two other adobes Vallejo built are gone. On east porch are old hand-carved pillars
ORANGE COUNTY *R. San Juan Cajon de Santa Ana Pioneer House		1857	Anaheim West & Sycamore Sts.	Open to public	Interesting collection of pioneer-day relics
Adobes: Avila, Burrel, Rios, Silvas, Valenzuela, Yorba		1794–1845	San Juan Capistrano Main St.	Homes & offices	Many adobe homes still left in quaint San Juan Capistrano
SACRAMENTO COUNTY *Sutter's Fort	John A. Sutter	1839–44	Sacramento Between K and H, 26th & 28th	Historical museum Open to public	Not only a fort but a trading post and place of refuge as well. Colonists given shelter, food, clothing and chance to work. John Sutter was important to settlement of the west

A GUIDE TO ADOBES AND LANDMARKS OF RANCHO DAYS

Rancho, Adobe, Landmark	Who Owned	When built	Where it is	Present Present	Interesting to know
SAN BENITO COUNTY					
*Castro Adobe	1st—José Castro Later—Patrick Breen of the Donner party	1835	San Juan Bautista Across plaza from Mission San Juan Bautista	State property Open to public Landmark 179	Home of Mexican governor. Good example of Monterey house
*Plaza Hotel	Patrick Breen	1840's	San Juan Bautista Next to Castro house	Open to public	Famous stopping place bet. Monterey and mines. Furnished as it was in those days
SAN BERNARDINO COUNTY					
*R. Rincon (Corner) Yorba-Slaughter Adobe	1st—Bernardo Yorba Later—Fenton Slaughter	1850	5 mi. S. of Chino on road to Prado	Landmark 191 Open to interested students	Stage used to stop on way to Yuma, Ariz. Home has original furniture
SAN DIEGO COUNTY					
R. Santa Fe	José María Osuña, 1st *alcalde* of San Diego; came with leather-jacket soldiers	1836	Hwy. 101, 3 mi. inland from Solano Beach	Home	Also called Rancho San Dieguito. Famous inn is on the old rancho
R. Guajome (Indian word for "frog")	1st—2 Indians Later—Abel Stearns, who gave it as wedding gift to Ysidora Bandini Couts	1845	3 mi. N.W. of Vista or 8 mi. E. of Oceanside	Home	Col. Cave Couts added to it; made 20 rooms. Very carefully preserved
R. Aguaje Hedionda (Stinking Water)	Juan Marron, sea captain	1840's	Road E. of Carlsbad off Hwy. 101, Grand to Chestnut, continue 6½ mi.	Leo Carrillo's "Ranch of the Spanish Daggers"	Also known as Kelly's Ranch
R. Santa Margarita	1st—Pio Pico and Andrés Pico Later—Juan Forster, their brother-in-law, of San Juan Capistrano	1828	Hwy. 101, 10 mi. N.E. of Oceanside	U.S. marine base, Camp Pendleton. Home is headquarters of general	One of the oldest and largest ranchos
R. Las Flores (The Flowers)	1st—Juan Forster Later—Louis Magee and Ruth Wolfskill de Magee	1868	Hwy. 101, ½ way bet. San Onofre & Oceanside, short distance inland from underpass	Home	Hospitality of this home has always been famous

A GUIDE TO ADOBES AND LANDMARKS OF RANCHO DAYS

Rancho, Adobe, Landmark	Who Owned	When Built	Where it is	Present use	Interesting to know
Casa de Bandini	Juan Bandini	1825	San Diego Old Town Cor. Mason & Calhoun, S.E. cor. of plaza	Apartment house	Once had only one story. Home was scene of many gay fiestas
*Casa de Carrillo	1st—Francisco Ruíz Later—Joaquín Carrillo	1807	San Diego Old Town N. side of Wallace bet. Juan & Sunset	Office of golf club	Oldest adobe in San Diego. Only small part of it left
*Casa de Estudillo	José Antonio Estudillo	1825	San Diego Old Town Mason St. bet. San Diego Ave. & Calhoun, across from plaza	Open to public Small charge	Furnished as it was in rancho days. Called "Ramona's marriage place" because of a story
*Casa de Machado	José Manuel Machado	?	San Diego Old Town Opp. W. gate of plaza	Machado Memorial Chapel	Machados were not sympathetic to Americans. Señora Machado cut down Mexican flag from plaza and ran into house with it before American soldiers came
*Casa de Pedroreña	Miguel de Pedroreña	1840	San Diego Old Town Around cor. from Casa de Estudillo	Restaurant	Pedroreña married his neighbor, María Antonia Estudillo
Whaley House	Capt. Thomas Whaley	1856	San Diego Old Town 2482 San Diego Ave.	Home	First brick house in San Diego. Plaster made from sea shells
Pendleton House	1st—Juan Bandini Later—Col. Geo. Pendleton	1852	San Diego Old Town 3877 Harney St.	Home	Don Juan Bandini gave it to his daughter as wedding gift
SAN LUIS OBISPO COUNTY					
R. Nipomo (Indian word for "foot of the hill")	William Dana	1835	Nipomo Turn N.E. at main intersection, road to left at top of hill	Home	Stopping place for travelers on El Camino Real. Famous for its hospitality
SAN MATEO COUNTY					
*R. San Pedro	Francisco Sanchez, *alcalde* and *comandante* of San Francisco	1846	Bet. Salada Beach & San Pedro Point, ¼ mi. E. of Hwy. 1	Owned by San Mateo County	Many famous guests entertained here

A GUIDE TO ADOBES AND LANDMARKS OF RANCHO DAYS

Rancho, Adobe, Landmark	Who Owned	When built	Where it is	Present use	Interesting to know
*R. Cañada de Raymundo (Woodside Store)	1st—Chas. Brown, whaler Later—Col. John Hays, 1st sheriff, San Francisco County	1854	La Honda Canyon, Portolá Rd., below junction with La Honda Rd., through gateway toward Searsville Lake	Museum Open to public Owned by San Mateo County	Charles Brown made shingles for George Yount of Napa
SANTA BARBARA COUNTY					
*Arrelanes Adobe	Teodoro Arrelanes	1795	Santa Barbara 800 Santa Barbara St.	Neighborhood House Assn.	Posts on porch brought from the large Aguirre home, now gone
*Carrillo Adobe	1st—Daniel Hill, who married Rafaela Ortega Later—José Antonio Carrillo	1826	Santa Barbara 11 E. Carrillo	Open to public Santa Barbara Foundation, gift of Max Fleischmann	First wooden floor in Santa Barbara. First American family lived here. Mrs. Larkin's child supposed to have been first American child born in Calif. (1833)
*Covarrubias Adobe	Domingo Carrillo, son of José Raimundo 1853—property of Joaquín Carrillo Later—José María Covarrubias (French)	1817	Santa Barbara 715 Santa Barbara St.	Headquarters of *rancheros visitadores*	Carrillo built for his bride, Concepción Pico. Original roof was made of tules, mud, tiles
*El Cuartel (Soldiers' Quarters)	Part of presidio	1782	Santa Barbara 123 W. Santa Barbara St.	Office of Boy Scouts	Santa Barbara's oldest adobe
*De la Guerra Adobe	José Julian de la Guerra y Noriega	1819–26	Santa Barbara 15-21 E. de la Guerra St.	Shops "El Paseo," Street of Spain	Scene of many social and political meetings
Rafael Gonzales Adobe	Rafael Gonzales	1825	Santa Barbara 835 Laguna St.	Home	Sometimes called Ramirez Adobe because Ramirez gave it to his daughter, who married Rafael Gonzales
Emil Goux Adobe	1st—María Antonio Feliz Later—Emil Goux, storekeeper	1812	Santa Barbara At rear of 1015 State St.	Home	Emil Goux tried to start silk industry in Calif. Brought in silkworms from China

A GUIDE TO ADOBES AND LANDMARKS OF RANCHO DAYS

Rancho, Adobe, Landmark	Who Owned	When Built	Where it is	Present use	Interesting to know
Masini Adobe	Pedro Masini	1820	Santa Barbara 20 Sheffield Dr., Montecito	Home	One of the first Monterey-style houses. Was once a stage stop
*Gaspar Oreña Adobes	Gaspar Oreña	1849–56	Santa Barbara Anacapa & De la Guerra	Shops	Part of one used as store-house for goods brought in from ships
*Captain Trussell Adobe	1st—Capt. Horatio G. Trussell Later—Winchester family	1853	Santa Barbara 412 W. Montecito	Santa Barbara Historical Soc.	Wood from wrecked ship used in house. Capt. Trussell came on first steamboat to enter Santa Barbara Harbor
R. Arroyo Hondo (Deep Creek) Vicente Ortega Adobe	Pedro and José Ortega	1840's	30 mi. N. of Santa Barbara, inland side of Hwy. 101	Home	Old stagecoach passed its doors. People stopped for food and rest from Santa Barbara to Lompoc
R. Tajiguas Kirk B. Johnson Adobe	Ortega family	1800	About 18 mi. N. of Santa Barbara, few miles inland on private road from Hwy. 101	Home	Rebuilt from ruins of Ortega home. Beautifully restored and kept
R. Najoque De la Cuesta Adobe	Dr. Ramon de la Cuesta	1851	W. side of Hwy. 101, just S. of Buellton	Home	Lumber brought on heads of oxen over Gaviota Pass because pass was too narrow for oxcarts
R. Los Alamos de Santa Elena (The Cottonwoods of Saint Helen)	1st—Don José Antonio, son of José de la Guerra y Noriega Later—His brother-in-law, Don Gaspar Oreña	1839	On former Hwy. 101, few mi. N. of Los Alamos	Home	Oreña brought his bride, Concepción Ortega, to this home. Adobe shows best of that day. One of the finest homes left of rancho days
*R. Guadalupe	Diego Olivera and Teodora Arrelanes	1849	Guadalupe	Meeting hall	Diego Olivera loved fine clothes and merrymaking. Arrelanes was called a "ranchero prince"
R. Los Cocheros (The Coachmen)	Daniel Hill	1830	Goleta 8 mi. N. of courthouse, on La Paterna Lane, ¼ mi. N. of Hwy. 101	Home	Part of Rancho Dos Pueblos (Two Towns). A place where visitors found a real welcome

121

A GUIDE TO ADOBES AND LANDMARKS OF RANCHO DAYS

Rancho, Adobe, Landmark	Who Owned	When Built	Where it is	Present use	Interesting to know
SANTA CLARA COUNTY R. Rinconada de los Gatos (Corner of the Cats)	José Hernandez and Sebastian Peralta	1840	Los Gatos Quito Rd., about 1 mi. N. of Austin Corners	Home	Part of present home built from old home
R. Milpitas (Little Cornfields)	Nicholas Berryessa and José María Alviso	1837	Milpitas Piedmont Rd., just S. of Calaveras Rd., 2 mi. E. of Milpitas	Home	Very well kept
R. de los Coches (The Pigs)	1st—Mission Indian Later—Antonio Suñol	1839–41	San Jose 770 Lincoln Ave.	Home	Today's adobe well preserved
*R. San José	One of old buildings of Mission Santa Clara	1779	San Jose 1067 Grant St.	Santa Clara Women's Club	Landmark 249
Peralta Adobe	Luis María Peralta	1804–08	San Jose 184 San Augustine	Warehouse	Part of old home still left. All of Peralta children born here
Burton Adobe	John Burton	1837	San Jose 247 S. Market St., S.W. cor. of old plaza	Home	He was first American to hold office in San Jose. Part of home left Santa Clara University
Fernandez Adobe	José Z. Fernandez	?	Santa Clara 401 Jefferson St.	Home	Once sold for $6.00 by Santa Clara to Fernando Berryessa and Francisco Bernal
R. Pastoria de los Borregas (Lamb's Pasture)	1st—Francisco Estrada Later—Martin Murphy	1849–50	Sunnyvale Sunnyvale Ave., nr. Calif. St.	Home	Home brought in pieces on ship from New England and put together in Calif. In early days boats bet. Alviso and San Francisco went by its bay side. El Camino Real was bet. the house and the bay. Now the main highway is on the back side. Sons helped found Santa Clara University
SANTA CRUZ COUNTY Arana Adobe	Manuel Arana	1849	Santa Cruz 47 Union St.	Home	Old wall is front of present home

A GUIDE TO ADOBES AND LANDMARKS OF RANCHO DAYS

Rancho, Adobe, Landmark	Who Owned	When Built	Where it is	Present use	Interesting to know
Alzina Adobe	Alzina family	1850's	Santa Cruz 8 Sylvar St.	Home	Lumber brought from mills near Pescadero
Blackburn Adobe	Wm. Blackburn	1845–47	Santa Cruz At head of Sycamore St.	Home	Blackburn, a Virginia cabinetmaker, became a lumberman, then county judge. Had famous orchards
Kirby Home	Richard Kirby	1850	Santa Cruz 129 Mission St., above Green St.	Home	Kirby born in England, left a whaling ship in Oregon and came to Calif. Went into tannery business. Kirby leather was famous. Imported rare shrubs and trees
*R. Bolsa del Pajaro (Bird's Nest)	Jesús Vallejo	1820	Watsonville N.W. side of Blackburn bet. 3rd & Lake Ave.	Girl Scout headquarters	Adobe brought from Rancho San Cayento on San Juan Rd. in Monterey
SHASTA COUNTY R. Buena Ventura (Good Fortune) Reading Adobe	Pierson B. Reading, partner of John A. Sutter of Sutter's Fort	1845–47	4 mi. E. of Cottonwood, W. bank of Sacramento River (or 3½ mi. S. of Ball's Ferry)	Home	Reading was among first to see gold found at Coloma. Home built with thick walls and high windows to protect family from Indian arrows. Around his fireplace, the builders of Calif. met—Sutter, Bidwell, Frémont. Here was grown the first cotton in the state
SOLANO COUNTY St. Catherine's Convent		1851	Benicia L St.	School & convent	It was first in Monterey, then moved to Benicia. Concepción Argüello was nun here
*State Capitol Building		1852	Benicia York & Sacramento	City Hall & Library	Landmark 153. Benicia was the third capital of the state, San Jose being first and Vallejo second

A GUIDE TO ADOBES AND LANDMARKS OF RANCHO DAYS

Rancho, Adobe, Landmark	Who Owned	When Built	Where it is	Present use	Interesting to know
SONOMA COUNTY *R. Cabeza de 　　Santa Rosa (Head of the 　Santa Rosa)	Francisca Carrillo	1841	Montgomery Village 2 mi. E. of Santa Rosa	Home Open to public	Francisca lived here with her unmarried children. Called "Mother Carrillo's House." Restored by Hugh B. Codding
R. Tzabaco (Indian word for 　"lost to history")	José Pina	1830	200 yds. off Redwood Hwy., 8 mi. N. of Healdsburg	Home	Built more like a fort than a home; had square portholes. Indians had *rancheria* near creek
*R. Agua Caliente (Hot Water) Tract 1	Mariano Vallejo	1850	Sonoma 3rd St.	Open to public Landmark 4	Lachryma Montis (Mountain Tears) and Swiss chalet are beautifully preserved homes of rancho days
*R. Petaluma	Mariano Vallejo	1834–44	4.3 mi. N.E. of Petaluma by D & Wilson Sts.	Historical landmark State of California	Home called Casa Grande (Large House). Largest adobe in Calif.
*Fort Ross	Russian settlement	1810–22	88 mi. N. of San Francisco	State Natl. Park	Where Russian settlers gathered rich fur harvest on land and sea. Sold to John Sutter
*Fitch House	Jacob B. Leese, brother-in-law of Vallejo	1840's	Sonoma 1st St. by plaza	Offices	Well preserved 2-story adobe
*Salvador Vallejo 　　　　Adobe	Salvador Vallejo	1840's	Sonoma Across from plaza	Shops	Home of Salvador, brother of Mariano Vallejo
*Blue Wing Hotel	Mariano Vallejo	1840	Sonoma Opp. Mission San Francisco de Solano	Open to public	Miners and bandit, Murietta, used to come here
*Bear Flag Monument		1846	Sonoma In plaza		Shows pioneer clutching the Bear Flag first raised in Sonoma plaza
*Soldiers' Barracks	Mariano Vallejo	1836	Spain St., across from plaza	Offices	Also headquarters for Bear Flag party

A GUIDE TO ADOBES AND LANDMARKS OF RANCHO DAYS

Rancho, Adobe, Landmark	Who Owned	When Built	Where it is	use	Interesting to know
TEHAMA COUNTY					
*R. de la Barranca Colorado (Red Bluff)	1st—Wm. B. Ide Later—Geo. Sutton	1846	2 mi. N. of Red Bluff	Landmark 12 State Park	Ide operated a ferry on Sacramento River known as Adobe Ferry. He had charge of Bear Flag Revolt in Sonoma
VENTURA COUNTY					
R. San Miguel Olivas Adobe	1st—Raymundo Olivas Later—Max Fleischmann	1841	3 mi. S. of Ventura, midway bet. Ventura & Santa Clara River bridges	Landmark 115 Private property	One of the best-preserved adobes. 21 Olivas children born here. Home famous for its hospitality
R. Camulos	Ignacio del Valle, *alcalde* of L. A.	1850's	16 mi. E. of Fillmore	Home	He had home by L.A. plaza until 1861. Travelers bet. missions always stopped here. Part of book *Ramona* written in this home
YOLO COUNTY					
R. Canada de Capay (Indian word for "stream")	1st—Francisco Berryessa Later—Geo. Stephens	1843–50	3 mi. W. of Capay, bet. Madison & Espartos	Home	Stephens built a large house around the first adobe
Gordon's Ranch	William Gordon trapper and hunter	1842	On Cache Creek, 10 mi. W. of Woodland	Home	Meeting place for settlers and hunters

adobe	ah-doh'-bay	unburned brick dried in the sun
alcalde	ahl-cahl'-day	mayor of the pueblo
Alvarado	Ahl-vay-rah'-do	governor of California
Amador	Ahm-ah-dohr'	early California family
Anza, Captain	Ahn'-zah	founder of San Francisco
Arguello	Ahr-gwehl'-yo	early California family
arroyo	ah-roy'-yo	a creek, dry most of the year
Avila	Ah'-vee-lah	early California family
ayuntamiento	ah-yuhn-tah-mee-ehn'-to	council or city government
Bandini	Bahn-dee'-nee	early California family
brea	bray'-ah	pitch, tar
buenos días	boo-eh'-nos dee'-ahs	good day
caballero	cah-bahl-yair'-o	horseman or gentleman
Cabrillo	Cahb-reel'-yo	First explorer of the California coast
camino	kah-mee'-no	highway or road
Camino Real	Kah-mee'-no Ray-ahl'	King's Highway or Road, path of the padres
carreta	kah-ray'-tah	oxcart with two large wooden wheels
Carrillo	Cahr-reel'-yo	early California family
casa	kah'-sah	house
cascarón	cas-cah-róhn	eggshell filled with perfume or bits of paper
Catalina	Cah-tah-lee'-nah	name of person and name of island
Cerritos	Say-ree'-tohs	little hills
comandante	ko-mahn-dahn'-tay	highest military title given by the Spanish in California
contradanza	kohn-trah-dan'-za	slow dance like a waltz
corral	ko-rahl'	pen for cattle or horses
corredor	cor-ray-dohr'	covered porch
Cota	co'-tah	early California family
cuartel	quar-tel'	a jail or soldiers' living quarters
Domínguez	Do-meen'-gwehs	early California family
Don	Dohn'	title of Spanish or Mexican gentleman
Doña	Dohn'-yah	title of Spanish or Mexican lady
Encarnación	Ehn-car-nas-cee-óhn	name of person
Estudillo	Es-too-dee'-yo	early California family
Eulalia	Eh-oo-lahl'-yah	keeper of the keys, San Gabriel Mission
Fages, Pedro	Fah'-hes Pay'-dro	leader of the leather-jacket soldiers
fandango	fan-dan'-go	festive Spanish dance or dancing party
fierro	fee-air'-oh	a range brand on hip of animal

126

fiesta	fee-es'-ta	a party or celebration
Flores	Flo'-rays	flowers, also name of general
frijoles	free-ho'-lehs	pink beans
Gabriel, San	Gah-bree-ale' Sahn	name of a mission and a valley
Guadalupe	Gwah-day-loo'-peh	name of person
Guerra, de la y Noriega	Gayr'-rah, day lah ee Nohr-ee-eh'-gah	name of family in Santa Barbara
hacienda	ah-see-end'-ah	smaller than a rancho; usually raised vegetables, not cattle
José	Ho-say'	Joseph
Josefa	Ho-say'-fah	Josephine
Los Angeles	Loce Ahng'-el-ess	city in southern California (the angels)
Lugo	Loo'-goh	early California family
Machado	Mah-cha'-do	early California family
madre	mah'-dray	mother
mañana	mah-nyah'-nah	tomorrow
mantilla	man-teel'-yah	lace shawl or veil that women wore over their heads
María	Mah-ree'-ah	Mary
Mariano	Mah-ree-ah'-no	first name of Vallejo
mayordomo	mah-yor-do'-mo	manager of a rancho
merienda	meh-ree-ehn'-dah	picnic
mesa	may'-sah	table or flatland
Monterey	Mon-tay-ray'	first capital of California
Neve, Felipe de	Nay'-vay, Fay-lee'-pay day	founder of Los Angeles
nuestra	noo-eh'-strah	our
Ortega	Or-tay'-gah	early California family
padre	pah'-dray	priest or friar
Palomares	Pahl-o-mah'-rays	early California family
palomino	pahl-o-mee'-no	cream-colored horse with white mane and tail
Paseo, El	Pay-say'-o, Ehl	the walk or pass
pastores	pas-tohr'-ays	shepherds
patio	pah'-tee-o	courtyard in center of house
Peralta	Pay-rahl'-tah	early California family
Pico, Pio	Pee'-ko, Pe'-o	last Mexican governor
piñate	peen-yah'-teh	jar or bag filled with sweets and gifts
plaza	plah'-sah	park
poblador	po-blah-dor'	founder or settler, citizen
poco tiempo	po'-co te-em'-po	after a while
Portolá	Por-toh-lah'	explorer

127

posada	po-sah'-dah	shelter or lodging
presidio	pray-see'-dyo	fort
pueblo	pway'-blow	town or village
Purísima, La	Poo-ree'-see-ma, Lah	mission
ramada (or enramada)	rah-mah'-dah	shelter made of tree branches
ranchería	rahn-chay-ree'-a	name given to Indian village
ranchero	rahn-chay'-ro	owner of a ranch
rancho	rahn'-cho	land granted by the Spanish and Mexican governments
reata	reh-ah'-tah	rope made of braided rawhide or horsehair
Refugio, El	Ray-foo'-hee-o, Ehl	Refuge, the (or shelter)
reina	ray-ee'-nah	queen
rodeo	ro-day'-o	roundup of cattle on a rancho
sala	sah'-lah	main room of a house, usually used for dancing
San Diego	Sahn Dee-ay'-go	name of a city
San Pascual	Sahn Pahs-kwahl'	name of a rancho
Santa Barbara	Sahn-ta Bahr'-bah-rah	name of a city and a mission
Sausal Redondo	Sah-oo-sahl' Ray-dohn'-do	round group of willows, name of a rancho
señor	say-nyor'	Spanish name for a man
señora	say-nyor'-ah	Spanish name for a woman
señorita	say-nyor-ee'-tah	Spanish name for an unmarried woman
Sepúlveda	Say-pool'-vay-dah	early California family
Serra, Father	Sayr'-rah	first founder of missions in California
siesta	see-ehs'-tah	nap after lunch
Solano	So-lah'-no	Indian chief in the north
Sonoma	So-no'-mah	city in the north
tortilla	tor-teel'-yah	flat, thin cake
tule	too'-lay	reed found in marshy land, used for roofs
Vallejo	Val-yay'-ho	early California family
vara	vah-'rah	about 50 yards
vaquero	vah-kay'-ro	cowboy
venta	vain'-tah	sale brand burned on shoulder when the animal was sold
Verdugo	Vayr-doo'-go	early California family
visitadores	vee-see-tah-dohr'-ehs	visitors
Yerba Buena	Ee-yer'-bah Boo-eh'-nah	sweet or good herb, first name given to San Francisco
Ygnacio	Ig-nahs'-see-o	name of person
Yorba	Ee-yor'-bah	early California family
zanja	san'-ha	ditch that brought water from the rivers
zanjero	san-hair'-o	caretaker of the zanja